Come Home Before Dark

Come Home Before Dark

*Selected Works From the COMPAS
Writers & Artists in the Schools Program*

Edited by
Sheila O'Connor

Illustrations by
Lauren Stringer

COMPAS
Writers & Artists in the Schools
1993

Publication of this book is generously supported by the Sven and C. Emil Berglund Foundation, dedicated in memory of C. Emil Berglund.

COMPAS programs are made possible in part by grants provided by the Minnesota State Arts Board, through an appropriation by the Minnesota State Legislature. In the past year, the COMPAS Writers & Artists in the Schools program has received generous support from the Hugh J. Andersen Foundation, the Ashland Oil Foundation, the First Bank System Foundation, the International Multifoods Charitable Foundation, Land O'Lakes and U S WEST Communications. COMPAS is an affiliate of United Arts.

As always, we are grateful for the hundreds of excellent teachers throughout Minnesota who sponsor COMPAS Writers & Artists in the Schools residencies. Without their support and hard work, the writers and artists would not weave their magic, and the student work we celebrate in this book would not spring to life.

For their work in producing this book, special thanks are due to Jo Svendsen, WAITS Program Associate; to Carol Bergelund, COMPAS Office Manager; and to Daniel Gabriel, WAITS Program Director.

ISBN 0-927663-21-X

Illustrations copyright © 1993 Lauren Stringer
Music, Additional Words, Arrangements copyright © 1993 Charlie Maguire and Mello-Jamin Music
Text copyright © 1993 COMPAS
All rights reserved. No portion of this book may be reprinted or reproduced without the prior written permission of COMPAS, except for brief passages cited in reviews.

COMPAS
305 Landmark Center
75 West Fifth Street
St. Paul, Minnesota 55102

Jeff Prauer, Executive Director
Daniel Gabriel, Director, Writers & Artists in the Schools

Table of Contents

Sheila O'Connor	*Introduction*	ix

I. Childhood Was Like This

Jennifer Warren	*New Pages*	2
Courtnie Dornfeld	*Special Things That I Remember from the Past*	3
Debbie Xiong	*When I Was Born*	4
Jacob Jensen	*Gonga*	5
Kira Levine Smith	*Little Teddy Doll*	6
Alex Vang	*Ode to My Baseball Glove*	7
Virginia Johnson's Class	*Be Q.T.*	8
Diane Arvidson's Class	*Scolding Poem*	9
Jong Yang	*People Teach Us Every Day*	10
Virginia Johnson's Class	*Calm*	11
Andy Acuff	*Memories*	12
Jolene Holthusen	*The Joy of Childhood*	13
Erica Gilberg	*An Electrician's Truck*	14
Lance Collman	*What I Learned*	15
Mai Lee	*Untitled*	16
Kelly Ritter	*Great-Grandfather's Basket*	17
Eric Paul	*Attack on Moo Company*	18

II. If You Want to Know Me

Tanya Starinets	*At The Edge of My Mind*	22
Sai Thao	*Let Me Never Become*	23
Jessica Gruenberg	*Untitled*	24
Kristi Hamlin	*Hopes and Dreams*	25
Tyler Olson	*I've Known*	26
Ryan Underbakke	*Spirithorse*	27

Sara Ennen	*The Colors of My Life*	28
Mai Xiong	*Life*	29
Andrew Karst	*Come With Me*	30
Matt Klug	*Anger*	31
Jon Nelson	*Fear*	32
Greg Hegedus	*Also Stubborn*	33
Marie Pogatschnik	*The Unforgettable Butterfly*	34
Sara Allen	*Lunchroom Terror*	35
Aisha Ghanchi	*Mix of the East and West*	36
Olivia Latimer	*Poem of Nature*	37
Brian Harms	*Bondage*	38

III. A Key That Can Open My Heart

Timmy Babatz	*Untitled*	40
Devon Urbanski	*The Gentle Tear*	41
Anna Curtis	*Sincerely*	42
Joe Burns	*My Mom*	43
Luther Flagstad	*Game Day*	44
David Saniti	*Who Is That Man?*	45
Keith Brown	*Leather Jacket*	46
Monica Wright	*Her*	47
Mike Olson	*My Sister*	48
Johnny Howard	*A Football Player Saying Bye Bye*	49
Amanda Grachek	*The Gift*	50
Mike Bradley	*To My Grandpa Laven*	51
Ryan Rasmussen	*Love Poem*	53
Rachel Beck	*Around the Fire Ring*	54
Nicholas Crisp	*The Hand That Unfolded Me*	55
Jason Bistodeau	*Untitled*	56
Travis Morrison	*The Love Story*	57
Amber Goetzke	*A Great Person*	58
Jesse Bewley	*My Friend Justin*	59
Teresa March	*The Captive*	60
Al Tripp's Class	*Group Play*	62

IV. So I Tell You Right Now, Good-Bye

Javon Jackson	*Untitled*	66
Becky Raasch	*Your Death*	67

Jessica DeYoung	*I Never Knew I Loved . . .*	68
Landis-Arvelia Harwell	*Arvelia*	69
Earl Tourville	*Old Arizona*	70
Beth Williams	*Moving*	72
James Adamiak	*Untitled*	73
Sarah Connelly	*Untitled*	74
Lolly Pederson's Class	*Anxious*	75
Becky Weets	*What a Tangled Web We Weave*	76
Joel Wertheim	*To My Uncle Carl*	77
Pacho Lara	*Forever Wasn't Enough*	78
Terra Pehl	*Why Did God Pick Me?*	79
Maggie McCormack	*The Dream is Over*	80
Stephanie Hickman	*Katie*	81
Peter Majerle	*The News—On the Death of Mike Olson*	82
Beth Knudsen	*The White Van*	83
Nicole Borgert	*Grandpa "Mac"*	84
Jan Gitter	*Untitled*	86
Devin M. Tkachuck	*Tribels*	87

V. WHERE MAGIC CAN SECRETLY HAPPEN

Angela K. Johnson	*James and Desire*	90
Sothara Has	*The Giant Step to Cambodia*	92
Bernadette Murphy	*Imagination*	93
Dena Gruber	*Ode to Laces*	94
Yen Dang	*The Heaven Land Book—excerpt*	95
Mary Beth D'Agosta	*A Crazy Poem to Read*	96
Anna Williams	*Mountain Secret, Mind Fire*	97
Natalie Homa	*Good Night, My Puppy*	98
Jennifer Workman	*Elisa's Dreams*	99
Liam McNally	*Five Minutes of Exercise*	100
Bob Axberg's Class	*Gotta Write!*	101
Shannon Nibbe	*Free Spirit*	104
Deon Klein	*Old Woman*	105
Margaret Mogck's Class	*The Desk*	106
Josh LaFond	*To My Guitar*	107
Betsy Murphy	*The Horse*	108
Hnou Moua	*I Am*	109
Kyle Swanson	*Let the Storms Come*	110

Henry Mundstock	*Untitled*	111
Shannon Rawson	*Arnold the Alligator*	112
Chris Collins' Class	*Group Play*	114
Jamie Miller	*Half Man Half Woman*	116

VI. MY PLACE IN THE WORLD

Ashley Thomas Kjos	*The Soft Side of Me*	118
Heidi McKay	*Nature*	119
Kelly Crandall	*How Lizard Changed Color*	120
Kelly Michels	*Bear*	121
Dustin Rosel	*Praise to Nature*	122
Ann Reidell's Class	*Sun Blue*	123
Heather Tichy, Jacob Richards, Jeff Sellman and Tara Stuntebeck	*Orangutans*	124
Colleen Hendrick	*Do You Know?*	125
Anya Scholl	*Ladyslipper*	127
Darla Heil's Class	*My Garden*	128
Songwriting Group	*Just Like Today*	129
Emily Gamble	*Arkansas*	131
Edward Burch, Jr.	*The Black Leopard*	132
Kim Oster	*I Am*	133
Louis Smeby	*White*	134
Bryan Shattuck	*Polished Works of Art*	135
Shannon Schulte	*The Place Where the Forest Doesn't Grow*	136
Kristi Schneider	*Watching*	137
Nicole Kliber	*My Cat Felix*	138
Cory Gross	*Love of Wilderness*	139
Erin Troutfetter	*My Place*	140

Author Index	141
School Index	145
Program Writers 1992–1993	149

Introduction

"My poem is a secret that cannot disappear."
       Henry Mundstock, Grade 2

There is a life to a poem, to a story, to our words, a life that transcends the moment of telling. We pass our messages on to each other, small parcels that others begin to carry in their minds and in their hearts. The amazing thing is, most of us have no idea where our words have traveled, no notion of the lives we've touched or changed.

A book is one way to honor the messages. It's a permanent thing, a solid piece of evidence that proves that our words are worth recording. And still the book lives beyond us as it makes its way quietly through the world, spreading our stories of hope, courage and love. I stand in front of a classroom in St. Paul, Minnesota. A room full of fifth graders have their eyes on me, waiting to hear the poem I hold in my hand. I begin by asking if they know where Belle Plaine, Minnesota is. A few do. Most don't. Nor do they know the young fourth grade poet whose poem speaks so eloquently of his parents' divorce. But there is a truth there, and the students feel as though someone unknown, in a small town far from them, has put into words exactly what divorce feels like. These strangers are united through the word, drawn together by the telling of a shared experience, and who knows how many years later one of my young St. Paul listeners will remember the line, "Divorce, you are a hurricane destroying my family."

In 1976, I was seventeen years old, standing in the bedroom of a new friend, a girl who had recently transferred to my small Catholic high school. She brought with her a worldliness, several years of hard living on the streets. She had something to show me. There on her dresser, under the clutter of make-up, perfume, hairbrush, bracelets and earrings, was her treasure: a collection of poetry written by students, people our age, who had worked with the COMPAS Writers-in-the-Schools program. We stretched out on her bed and read, her favorites marked with torn scraps of paper. She said a poet had come to her old school and taught her the importance of writing about her life. She said the poetry changed her. I was astonished. A real poet. School time devoted to poetry. I had spent my childhood filling notebooks with my poems and stories, but never had I met a real writer, someone who could tell me that what I wrote mattered. Suddenly, there was this book written by people like me; for the first time I realized the possibility of actually having someone, far away, read my words. At that moment, I began a dream; someday, I would be the writer coming into the classroom of students, telling them to value their lives through poems and stories.

Eighteen years later, in classrooms across Minnesota, I stand in front of students and read them poems from the COMPAS anthologies. They listen carefully, every word stored in their memories as something worth saving. They say, "That was written by a third grader!" "How did they get in that book?" "Would they ever publish something by me?" When I'm sharing work by their peers, a sense of empowerment moves through the classroom, a boost of confidence: "I can write, too." "I can tell my stories and my poems, and they will matter." "My work is worth reading." To be heard, to know someone is listening, is a universal longing. Putting our words down on paper, seeing them in print, acknowledges the value of written communication. Every book is a celebration of our continued connection through language. A book is one way to make sure our poems won't disappear.

There are children all over Minnesota who have given others the great gift of their experience through the COMPAS Writers & Artists in the Schools program, thousands of children who don't appear in this book. But published or not, their poems continue to live in the writers who met them, and in their fellow students, who know them a little better by just listening to what they had to say. When I go into a classroom I carry a stack of poems with me, poems to share with the students, poems to inspire them to write. I carry the messages from Minneapolis, Long Prairie, Hopkins and Moorhead. And when I leave each classroom, I add their new poems to my collection. And in this way, the COMPAS writers are weaving a thread of expression and understanding throughout the state.

What children have to say is important. This is the conviction that the COMPAS writers bring to every residency; it's the belief that inspires this book. In January, driving through a snowstorm to an elementary school in Shakopee, I listened to President Clinton give his inaugural address. He spoke of the future of our nation, he spoke of the children. And there, in the front seat of my car, stuffed into my huge black bag was some of the most important information any President would need. The experience of a child, in the words of a child. I wanted to send him a COMPAS anthology with a note that read, "Pay attention. The most important things are in here."

And that's what I ask of you. Pay attention. The most important things are in here.

Sheila O'Connor
July, 1993

A Note to Teachers

Using *Come Home Before Dark* as Source Material for Writing

Come Home Before Dark is a powerful collection of writing which expresses the passions, concerns, dreams and experiences of students throughout Minnesota. Using these stories and poems as models will inspire young writers to put their own lives into words. Moreover, it will give them the confidence to communicate through writing.

The possibilities for incorporating these poems and stories into your writing curriculum are endless. The thematic sections of this anthology will allow you to find work dealing with specific subjects. Begin with the pieces you think will engage your class. For example, you may choose a praise poem to encourage your students to celebrate a season, a place, an occasion. Or you could use some of the animal pieces included in this collection, asking the students to write from the voice of a wolf, a bear, an endangered species. Friends? Families? Try sharing some of the portrait poems and ask them to write about someone significant in their lives. How about memories? Read the poems about childhood. Ask them to write about their own experience. Sometimes you can use just a line to get the students started (I am the poet who. . .) or a single image that captures your attention. Then, the students can brainstorm, create a new piece from a shared fragment. If it's elements of good writing you want to model (metaphor, simile, imagery, description, detail) this collection is full of some fine examples.

Finally, let them page through it. Let them read work by writers like themselves, so they will see and believe that not only is it possible, it is also important.

Childhood Was Like This

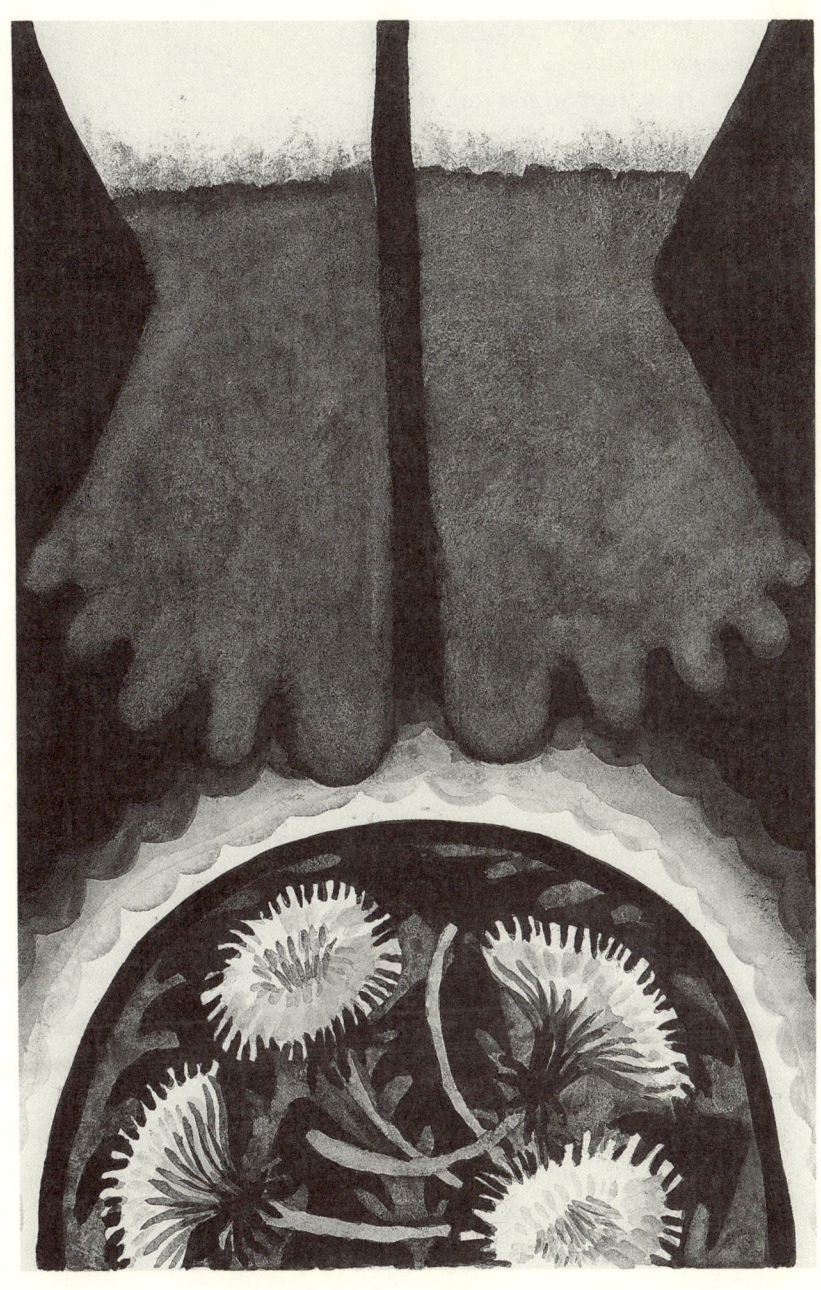

New Pages

Childhood is like a new notebook
with its pages full of life.
As you grow older,
the pages are written on and torn out.
You become an adult
when your childhood is all written out,
and the only things that remain
are the scraps of memory,
floating around inside.

Jennifer Warren :: Grade 5
Tanglen Elementary School :: Hopkins

Special Things that I Remember from the Past

Ugly-named-girl-born summer
My-first-polite-year summer
Ninja-loving-brother-born summer
First-Christmas-that-I-sang-solo winter
Dress-up-and-trip-on-fireplace spring
Ran-to-bathroom-and-hit-wall-got-stitches summer
Thought-barbie-doll-kidnapped spring
Learned-how-to-do-a-cartwheel winter
Taking-pictures-of-dolls-wtih-dad's-camera winter
Cute-funny-half-brother-born summer

Courtnie Dornfeld :: Grade 5
Chelsea Heights Elementary School :: St. Paul

When I Was Born

When I was born, nothing
much happened. All except
that Dad wasn't there, all except
granny who didn't know
how to keep her mouth shut.

When I was born, the Twins
didn't win the World Series.
Everybody watched but me.
It was hard to get out
and I missed it.

When I was born, our sponsors
came to see me with my bottle,
sucking and sucking and sucking.

When they took me home
the colors I saw were blue and
white. From then to now they
are my favorite colors.

The year I was born, it
was boring until I got some
toys to play with.

When I was a couple of years old,
Sesame Street and Mr. Rogers
were on TV. Sometimes I miss it,
but my little brother keeps me
up to date.

Debbie Xiong :: Grade 5
Parkway Elementary School :: St. Paul

Gonga

Oh Gonga
your fur is like nothing I have felt before.
You have love through the years.

Oh Thumb Sucker
you have made me remember when I was a baby.
I remember when I would not go anywhere
without you.

Oh Little Rip in the Arm
I was playing when you came.

Oh Little Monkey
I do not know what I would do without you.

Oh Little Foot
you are so cute.
Your eyes are like little stars.

Jacob Jensen :: Grade 2
Oakridge Elementary School :: Eagan

Little Teddy Doll

Good night little
teddy doll. The sun
is asleep. The moon
is awake. I love
you teddy doll. We
love the stars in
the sky. Good night
teddy doll. Good night.

Kira Levine Smith :: Grade 2
Webster Magnet School :: St. Paul

Ode to My Baseball Glove

My baseball glove is always
on my bed,
pale and brown
as Lamont's brown
bear. When I
catch with it
it feels like I was
in the World Series,
and I just won it
too. When I put my hand in it
it feels like if I
put my hand in a
hollow tree. It
feels good when I
put my hand in
that glove. When I
don't use it and
I see it on the bed pole
it looks lonely, so I
go play catch with
it and afterwards it
looks as if it was
having fun.

Alex Vang :: Grade 5
Parkway Elementary School :: St. Paul

Be Q.T.

Be Q.T.
    Be soft and fuzzy and cuddly.
    Be friendly.
    Don't poop on the rug.
    Be happy—jump around in circles.

Be Q.T.
    Don't nibble on paper and books.
    Play with us kids!
    Eat carrots.
    Stay cute.

Be Q.T.

Virginia Johnson's Class :: Kindergarten
Parkway Elementary School :: St. Paul

Scolding Poem

Don't talk to strangers, Rita.
Don't smoke, Youa.
Don't talk to rocks, Nathan.
Read a book, Leng.

Stop going into the street, Tong.
Stop throwing rocks at cars, Jimmy.
Clean off the table, Amanda.

Don't play with guns, Choua.
Don't push in line, Nick.
Don't cross the street by yourself, Serina.
Holly, don't burn down houses.

Don't throw snowballs outside, Deon.
Don't play with a knife, Elizabeth.
Don't start a fight, Andy.
Song, don't touch the fish.

Clean up, Bernard.
Wash up, Deon.
Wash the dishes, Choua.
Be cool, stay in school, Justin.

Diane Arvidson's Class :: Grade 1
Parkway Elementary School :: St. Paul

People Teach Us Every Day

I remember when I wrote on the wall.
I remember when my sister taught me to write my name.
I remember when I wrote my name on my sister's door with a red marker.
I remember when my mom went to sleep and I colored my sister's windowshade.
I remember when I wrote on my shoe.
I remember when I wrote on my hand. I thought it would look pretty.

Jong Yang :: Grade 3
Chelsea Heights Elementary School :: St. Paul

Calm

Calm rabbits
Calm babies
When me and Margie ride bikes, we be calm
Calm bears
Calm birds
Calm dinosaurs
Calm clothes
Q.T. is calm when we pet her
Calm lipstick—they just sit there
Goats are calm
Jogging and playing at the school playground makes us calm
When me and Mark go to school
and play with hard puzzles together, we are calm.

Sometimes we like to be wild.
Sometimes we like to be calm.

Virginia Johnson's Class :: Kindergarten
Parkway Elementary School :: St. Paul

Memories

I remember my mom looking for my sister when she's really in the cow pen when it's rainy out. I can see myself with my old dog Snowball playing catch and tug-a-war. I can smell my grandma's homemade turkey dinner. I feel my hand against my old dog Snowball's back. I can hear my mom calling my name to wake me up. I can see my dad working on our truck. I can feel my hands getting greasy helping him. I can hear my mom telling me to wash my hands. I remember when we had a flood. I feel the rain water on my hot face. I can taste my mom's homemade chocolate chip cookies. I can see her putting the chocolate chips in the dough. I can hear my cat meowing at the birds and running into our kitchen window. I remember in the third grade my best friend Craig died because he and his brother were horsing around and he fell into a wheat auger. I remember waking up to the Channel 5 News saying, "An exclusive story of a young boy getting caught in an auger. His name was Craig Piney."

Andy Acuff :: Grade 6
Parkway Elementary School :: St. Paul

The Joy of Childhood

Childhood was like this
    It was the feel of mud squishing up through
      my toes
    Falling from an oak tree into a soft bank of
      snow
    Running deer
    Singing crickets
    Joy.

Childhood was
    Running barefoot through dew-soaked grass.
    The crack of a bat and the shattering of
      glass.
    Playing poor.
    Fuzzy kittens.
    Happiness.

Childhood was
    Homemade fishing poles with corn-baited hooks.
    The smell of wild roses pressed neatly in books.
    Loosely hung clotheslines.
    Dandelion soup
    Contentment.

Jolene Holthusen :: Grade 12
Roseau High School :: Roseau

An Electrician's Truck

I would climb into Dad's truck,
sitting high on the seat.
The scent of that truck
I would recognize as Dad's.
I can't describe this.
It was just my dad,
his defined face
strong and loving,
his scratchy stubble
that would tickle our feet,
his rough hand
gripping my tiny one.
When I climbed into that front seat,
I would always twist
to see jumbled
tools, wires and ladders,
more scrambled
than the toys and clothes
on the floor of my room.
I would hear
the big old truck grumble
as he flipped the golden key
with that magic our parents had.
I would feel
the body of the truck
shaking,
as we started forward,
bouncing and jiggling away
down the dusty dirt road.

Erica Gilberg :: Grade 9
Stillwater Junior High School :: Stillwater

What I Learned

I learned to drive
the tractor in second grade.
    I learned that you can't
have everything you want.
I learned to eat a corn dog
but not like them.
    I learned not to waste
my money on video games.
I learned that my cousin
was not my brother.
    I learned how
to blow my nose, brush my teeth.
I learned how
to use a chain saw.
    I learned how to milk
a cow and ignore the turkey
so he leaves you alone.
I learned to walk
before I could crawl.
    I learned how to make
kool-aid in second grade.
I learned not everything is easy
and to accomplish things
without giving up.
That's the best I learned.

Lance Collmann :: Grade 5
Callaway Elementary School :: Callaway

Untitled

Springtime flowers are blooming
Children are moving
Like butterflies in the sky.

Mai Lee :: Grade 5
Hayden Heights Elementary School :: St. Paul

Great-Grandfather's Basket

My great-grandfather once owned a basket. It cost almost $400.

My great-grandfather kept it on the table in his family room. He kept it there so everyone could see it. But one day my two brothers Mike and Joe were playing catch at his house, hit the basket and it cracked. Mike said, "Joe, what are we going to do? We cracked great-grandpa's basket."

"We could glue it," said Joe.

"No," said Mike, "Let's hide it in the closet."

"OK," said Joe, and they did.

When their great-grandpa got home from the store, he noticed the basket was not on the table. So he asked Mike and Joe what they did with the basket.

Mike said, "I don't know."

But Joe confessed and told their great-grandpa what they did with the basket. They only got grounded for one week.

Kelly Ritter :: Grade 5
Birch Grove Elementary School :: Brooklyn Park

Attack on Moo Company

One very hot afternoon Billy and I went for a walk and came upon a very strange smell that neither I nor Billy had smelled before. I for one didn't know what it was for I was only seven years old at the time, and Billy had no idea either because he was only eight years old and was dumber than a box of rocks. All I know is that it was part of our fun for the day.

The day started out when I came over to Billy's house to play. I came over all dressed up like a soldier ready to go to war. I had my trusty play lever-action pop gun, green army clothes on, and twine string all tied together for a rope. Billy also was dressed as a soldier, but had a black noise-making handgun instead of a rifle. We made our plans silently in our cardboard headquarters by the barn. We planned to travel along the main highway of the woods which simply was a tractor path that traveled all over the woods down to the river and some hay fields. We planned on attacking Moo Company by following the highway looking for any sign of where they may be. They were as big as horses, but were covered with big black and white spots. They moved very carefully through the woods while trying to take over our headquarters by the barn. We knew it was going to be tough to defeat Moo Company, but we had to do it to save our headquarters.

"All ready to go Private," Bill said to me.

"All ready to go Sergeant," I replied. So we left silently in search of Moo Company. We slowly followed the highway keeping our eyes open for any sign of Moo Company. We kept on slowly walking for about a fourth of a mile until we came to a very thick patch of blackberries. Here we started to eat some of the juicy berries when it hit.

I asked, "Do you smell something strange in the air?"

"Yea, now that you mention it," replied Billy. I started to slowly look around with my eyes, but my nose led my face in the correct direction.

"Sergeant, I think we better move our position right now. Look to your left just on the other side of that red oak tree about fifty feet away," I said.

Billy turned his head and yelled, "Let's move it right now!" Right there before us was a small creature. It consisted of white and black stripes with its tail pointing like a cannon at us. We both became deer right there and took off down the highway. Finally, we had to slow down and remember our assignment.

"Want to stop here by the split?" Billy asked.

"OK," I replied. We stopped at the split in the road to make a very important decision. Because the right path leads down to the river while the left path leads to some hay fields.

"Well, I think Moo Company will be down around the river refreshing themselves," I said.

"After we catch our breath, let's go down there," answered Billy.

We got our breath and bearings back and headed out to the river by following the path. We slowly moved along keeping our eyes, ears, and nose open for any sign of Moo Company or other white and black cannon animals. After we had gone about two hundred feet we came upon a football field-sized meadow that ran down the side of a hill to the river. This made it difficult to cross for if we were seen by Moo Company it would spoil our surprise attack.

"Why don't you scan the area, Private, for Moo Company," said Billy. So I put my hand binoculars on and scanned the area. I looked all over the meadow and didn't see a thing except the river and a small sandy beach. To the right of us at the side of the meadow was brush that was so dense it was as dark as night except for a highway leading through it. We began crawling on our bellies like snakes in high grass. After we snaked along for twenty feet we stopped and took our positions and waited for Moo Company to come. Then it happened.

"Do you hear something," I asked.

"Yea, it sounds like a machine. Why don't you get out your binoculars," said Billy. So I quickly surveyed the area and then I noticed them.

"Here comes Moo Company with one red International moo vehicle right behind them!" I yelled.

"Fire away!" said Billy.

I kept firing my trusty rifle while Billy fired his noisy hand gun. "Sergeant, they're outflanking us on the right. We'll be surrounded if we don't retreat," I said.

"I agree," said Billy.

We quickly retreated back twenty running steps to a group of boulders that were oversized marbles. They kept on coming closer and closer. We kept firing and firing. Then the battle was turned. For they saw how powerful we were and turned up the highway we came down. The armored moo vehicle though kept coming and coming until it was upon us. We were shaking in our boots afraid of what might happen next. Then the vehicle stopped.

"You boys want a ride back to the barn?" asked the driver. We surrendered and rode back to camp.

Eric Paul :: Grade 12
Long Prairie High School :: Long Prairie

If You Want to Know Me

At The Edge of My Mind

At the edge of my mind
silver highways hurry like wind.
I should be where I belong,
but I'm stuck here, like a rock
laying in one place.
At the edge of my mind,
tiny blue branches in the night
play a thrilling melody.
I should be friends
with the popular kids,
who do what they want,
but instead I hurry like wind
somewhere where I'm needed and loved.
At the edge of my mind,
the wind changes night into silver.
I see the changes occur.
It looks like lightning
without any noise.
At the edge of my mind,
highways like melodies
run before my eyes.
They're like a non-stop circle
going around and around.
That's what I once was,
that's what I still am.

Tanya Starinets :: Grade 7
Hopkins West Junior High School :: Hopkins

Let Me Never Become

Let
me never become
lonely
like a pond
with no water
Let me never
become
a house
without a roof
Let
me never
become a
book without
pages
Let me
never become
sad
as the moon
Let me
never
become a girl
with no voice
Let me become
a lovely bird
with a beautiful
voice in the air

Sai Thao :: Grade 6
Parkway Elementary School :: St. Paul

Untitled

Open the curtains
lie on my side
I fall asleep.

In the middle
of the night
my hands
wake up

and remember
moving like
a ballerina

and swimming
through a pond
like a fish

they become
a root and
move into the
soil

and become a
blossom.

Jessica Gruenberg :: Grade 3
Aquila Primary Center ·· St. Louis Park

Hopes and Dreams

My hopes run free like a waterfall.
They are as wild as a wolf and
fly like an eagle in the night
sky. But sometimes they are shadowed,
secret and alone. But sometimes
they are lost in the past or the
future. They are like a river
flowing free on its own. My hopes
and dreams are as special as a
gemstone in the middle of a fire.

Kristi Hamlin :: Grade 5
Kingsland Elementary School :: Spring Valley

I'VE KNOWN . . .

I've known waterfalls older than the
ancient dinosaurs that roamed the earth,
and older than the first blazing flames
of fire.

I've known oceans that stretch
farther than the Great Plains of central
America, and deeper than a person's
sorrow.

I've seen streams evaporate faster
than a sonic boom, and faster than
the population of mankind has grown.

I've seen a tear wiped away by
a single stroke of a tissue, and seen
it swept away just as the Indians
were swept from their land.

I've seen time tick away faster
than the world record of any
runner or automobile, and faster than
the days, months and years pass by.

I've known waves stronger than an
oxen that works in the fields of a
farmer, and swifter than an eagle
sweeping down after its prey.

Tyler Olson :: Grade 6
Crestview Elementary School :: Cottage Grove

Spirithorse

I am spirithorse
grace and power
by the hour.

Speed is my brother.
My soul never really dies,
it lives in another body for eternity.

My name came from Australia
and means truthful.
My soul never really dies.

It lives forever.
I glide from the past,
I am only a boy named Ryan.

A warrior's name it is,
because of the power
it brings to the mind.

But spirithorse
will always be
inside me . . . always

Ryan Underbakke :: Grade 4
Harriet Bishop Elementary School :: Rochester

The Colors Of My Life

Blue, my moon is the seed
 of beauty.

Marigold, my sky is the neverending
 story of life.

Black, my life is the shatter
 of love poems.

Gold, my future lights up
 the world.

Silver, my joy is hidden in
 the south seas.

Scarlet, my love beholds
 the future.

Sara Ennen :: Grade 5
Elm Creek Elementary School :: Maple Grove

Life

I am a chicken
    laying eggs.
I am a mouse
    that someone has memories of.
I am the sound of waterfalls, that
    falling down to meet the river.
I am a house
    that has memories and stay in place.
I am the moon, whose
    talking to the night.
I am the sun
    talking to the dawn.
I am the wind
    who is always lonely.
I am a smell
    that comes from a pie.
I were you and you are me
    but who are the people around us?
I am the taste of candies and sweets.
I am Angie that
    nobody knows.
I am Little Mai
    who everybody knows.
I am a girl
    who was small but happy at birth.

Mai Xiong :: Grade 6
Parkway Elementary School :: St. Paul

Come With Me

I come from a house
that gets dirtier every day
from us tracking in mud.
I come from a family that is nice to me.
If you want to know me
you need to come climb trees
with me, fish with me.
You have to dream my dreams,
scary dreams, terrifying dreams.
You have to come fly with me,
sink with me,
float with me,
do everything with me.
Come with me.

Andrew Karst :: Grade 6
Gordon Bailey Elementary School :: Woodbury

Anger

Anger, I need your fire
too much happiness
I need your black vulture
my house fire red
the ruby is shattered
I need your fire
the mystic is gone
the ammo port is full
I need your fire
I need your dark hat
Anger, help me.

Matt Klug :: Grade 7
Caledonia Junior High School :: Caledonia

Fear

Tonight I'd be afraid to dream about . . .
Going back to the dark city.
Being worried somebody might jump out of a shadow,
With gleaming eyes and gleaming blade.
Being worried that when I leave my car,
That it won't be there when I return.
That I might take a stray bullet,
Aimed at someone else,
Walking down a dark alley.
That someday my sister might
Come home bruised and beaten,
Only because someone didn't like the way she looked.
Tonight I'd be afraid to dream about the city.

Jon Nelson :: Grade 12
Bemidji High School :: Bemidji

Also Stubborn

When I sculpt myself I
fall apart like dry sand.

When my mother sculpts me I
stay like leather, dried and stiff.

She sculpts me well, I
appreciate her.

Yet today I sculpted myself and I
stayed together like
atoms frosted together
in a molecule.

I feel great,
a stone so great that
can't be broken.

Greg Hegedus :: Grade 5
Alice Smith Elementary School :: Hopkins

The Unforgettable Butterfly

I am the butterfly that looks like glass.
I go through you like a knife through
your hourglass. I eat your "q," "z," "x"
as you write them in school. I am
like a thunderstorm about to
streak the lightning low enough to touch
the cold, wet, hard ground. I am as dry
as a lump of pink ink. I live in your bedroom
closet as quiet as rain. You come with me
in your dreams across a rose-filled field. I am
like your mom calling you to come home
before dark.

Marie Pogatschnik :: Grade 4
Holdingford Elementary School :: Holdingford

Lunchroom Terror

Words are spoken
but not to me.
Unspoken words seem to hover
over me
like the hazy perfume
that surrounds some ladies too thickly.
The stillness of being alone
in a crowd of people
sweeps over me.
My face feels toasted hot
and seems to be painted carnation pink.
I stare blindly
at the sea of people
sitting all around me
in island-like clusters.

Sara Allen :: Grade 10
Grand Rapids High School :: Grand Rapids

Mix of the East and West

He wants me to wear whatever I want
as long as it's not shorts

He wants me to talk on the telephone
as long as it's one of the girls

He wants me to be social and friendly
as long as I come home with an A

He wants me to dance and have lots of fun
as long as it's a fast dance

He wants us to visit and share thoughts
as long as it's not during the 10 o'clock news

He wants me to know a man can cook
as long as I know it's nice for a woman too

He wants me to be strong and brave without fear
as long as I come to him when I need comfort

He wants me to be independent and make my own decisions
as long as I don't forget I'm still his little girl

He wants me to question anything or anyone
as long as I follow through

He wants me to speak my mind
as long as it's at the right time

He wants me to pursue my dream as a lawyer
as long as I don't argue with him

He wants me to be a successful woman
and he wants me to believe in who I am

Aisha Ghanchi :: Grade 7
Blake Middle School :: Hopkins

Poem of Nature

My dreams are huge overgrown ladybugs flying from leaf to leaf. My dreams are huge wolves chasing deer. The breeze of my dreams carries ghosts to town. The snow of my dreams comes down and covers me under the sky like a blanket. My dreams are tears flowing down my face. My dreams are lakes with people swimming and tubing. My dreams are tidal waves flowing over the shore. My dreams are the green of grass and trees. My dreams are the orange of Halloween and pumpkins. My dreams are the blue of the sky and water. My dreams are seas full of fish.

Olivia Latimer :: Grade 2
Warba Elementary School :: Warba

Bondage

"and if you integrate using Simpson's rule . . ." I groan softly as the professor's grating voice punishes my ears again. How much longer do I have to bear this classroom; how much longer until I am insane?

An endless row of desks, scraping painfully against the floor as students sit up, provides a pathway for the light coming off the teacher's bald head to hit me like a spotlight. Overhead hanging lights swing slowly in the oppressively warm breeze sifting through open windows.

The sounds of stop-and-go traffic on the street below dull my brain to example after tedious example on the board. The bare white walls press in on me—trapping me.

Even worse is the smell of fresh graphite scraping onto fresh paper by attentive kids with ramrod straight backs. Don't they have anything better to do than learn? Can't they taste the freedom outside?

Suddenly I am aware of ceiling fans blowing humid air down on my suffocating head. I feel like my clothes are sticking to me, and me to my chair. The fans move in coordinated motion—endlessly, calmly turning. They seem to slow as I look at them, extending my torture in this horrible room!

"How much longer?" I wonder aloud. My voice echoes throughout the room, cutting the intense air like a knife. I attempt to stretch in my seat, but my legs are burning, twitching, convulsing against the overwhelming weight of formulas and unwanted knowledge.

Everything grinds, smashes, destroys me—everything I see, hear, feel. It cuts my soul into oblivion. I lower myself yet again under the newspaper's cover and immerse myself in rows of box scores.

Brian Harms :: Grade 11
Prior Lake High School :: Prior Lake

A Key That Can Open My Heart

Untitled

Will you love me
when we don't know
each other anymore?
Will you love me
when all elephants
are dead? Will you love
me when the fawns
lose their spots?
Will you love
me when I kick
my shoes off?
Will you love
me when the shaggy
dog turns into a camel?
Will you love me
when you are
an old lady?

Timmy Babatz :: Grade 1
Aquila Primary Center :: St. Louis Park

The Gentle Tear

If I am the stars that shine at night, my mom
is the heart that fills me with love.
If I am the tear, my dad is the cloth that wipes
the tear away.
If I am the rose, my brother
is the grass that I am planted in.
If I am the rain, my uncle is the
clouds that bang together making
the thunder.
If I am the memory, my grandma
is the mind that keeps the memory in.
If I am the morning bird, my friend
is my voice that wakes up the people.
If I am the pillow, my grandpa is
the feathers that are in the pillow.

Devon Urbanski :: Grade 4
Madison Elementary School :: Blaine

Sincerely

Even before I could remember
Your voice was there
Soothing, mellow, comforting
Your voice is so much older than you.
You have a crooked smile
the smile of a gypsy
Your hands are rough and work-worn
the hands of an artist.

Anna Curtis :: Grade 7
Blake Middle School :: Hopkins

My Mom

You are a breeze that blows me down.
A teacher that makes me learn.
An ice cream cone that can change into different
flavors. A light that shines on me.

You are a butterfly that takes me places.
A volcano about to erupt when I do something wrong.
A bird who pecks at my window.
A key that can open my heart.

You are magic that can make me clean.

Joe Burns :: Grade 5
Pullman Elementary School :: St. Paul Park

GAME DAY

Here is my dad throwing a football for me
to catch.
I am not a good football player!
My dad throws the football to me.
Oh no! I dropped it!
I feel just like an embarrassed football player
missing a perfect pass.
I remember when that happened in the Super Bowl.
I pick it up and throw it back to my dad.
It is NOT an accurate throw!
My dad makes a diving leap and catches it!
My dad gets up.
He has grass stains on his jeans.
He has grass in his hair.
My dad is smiling.
I'm trying to smile too, but my smile isn't very
big or strong.
My dad looks just like a football player
working as hard as he can.
My dad says I'll help you learn to throw and catch!
Really! I say excitedly.
Sure, my dad says. GREAT!!!
See ya tomorrow!

Luther Flagstad :: Grade 3
Chelsea Heights Elementary School :: St. Paul

Who Is That Man?

Are you having
a good time?
A man would say.
These walls look
nice, that man would say.
Mighty fine house,
That man would say.
Let's go eat,
That man would say.
What would you
like? That man
would say.
Who was that man?
Oh, what do
you know, it was
my dad.

David Saniti :: Grade 4
Edgerton Elementary School :: Maplewood

Leather Jacket

The smell of
leather
reminds me of my
dad's freshly washed
Harley
screaming down the
interstate like an
eagle
chasing its prey.
The smell of the
exhaust is like
a charging bull
puffing
through his nose.
The excitement of
the wind in my
face all because
of the leather jacket
I wear.

Keith Brown :: Grade 7
Oltman Junior High School :: St. Paul Park

Her

She was the one who threw a heel in my eye.
She was the one who tore my new shirt.
She told my mom that I spilled her juice.
She was the one who kissed the first boy.
She was the one to get the best looks.
She was the one to be most energetic,
the one who wrote on her wall,
the one to be the most popular of all.
She was the one to get my old teachers.
She was the one to like all the foods.
She was the one to get all the attention.
She was the one, my little sister.

Monica Wright :: Grade 6
North End Elementary School :: St. Paul

My Sister

I remember when I first wheeled
my handicapped sister
down the driveway,

when my sister Jeni
said my name, Mikey.

I remember the first time
I taught my sister Jeni to give
me a high five and thumbs up,

to count to three and how to stand
up using the railing.

I remember the time I first
took Jeni outside to play
with her toys,

the time when Jeni scooted
to the TV to look at Big Bird.

I remember the time I got
Jeni a big Barney stuffed animal
for Christmas and she played
with it every day

and when I learned she had
cerebral palsy

I remember her first seizure
and I hope she always remembers me.

Mike Olson :: Grade 6
Highwood Hills Elementary School :: St. Paul

A Football Player Saying Bye Bye

My brother is
learning how to
talk.
My brother only says
words like bubbles,
hot, eat, juice, and
bye. My brother
brings me to the
bubbles and says
bubbles. Then when
it is time to eat
he says eat like a
tape recorder.
When it is time to go,
he pushes everybody
out the door like
a football player
blocking, saying bye, bye.

Johnny Howard :: Grade 4
Chelsea Heights Elementary School :: St. Paul

The Gift

Somewhere I can remember
a time long ago
when sitting on my grandpa's lap
he would tell a story
while holding me close
or we'd play chase.

Now I'm much older,
no more stories,
no more chase.
Even though those
times are gone
my grandpa still says,
"Little Babe."

Every time I hear that I know it's my grandpa
because only he calls me
"Little Babe."

Out in his workshop filled with tools,
the sound of his hammer
like the pounding of thunder.
I see him, plaid shirt,
worn out blue jeans,
cigar in his mouth,
pounding away.

He's at it for an hour
or two, then with a
wet red face he says,
"Little Babe,
come on out."
So I come out to see
why he calls my name
with loving tenderness.

Then I see why,
the best gift
in the world,

His Heart.

Amanda Grachek :: Grade 6
St. Michael Elementary School :: St. Michael

To My Grandpa Laven

You are like the space in a square
>that makes it whole.
You are the la in a laugh.
You are like emeralds
>so shiny.
Your voice is like a siren
>reaching everyone.
You are like the ham on Easter
>always the center of attention.
You are like the lion
>strong but with feeling.
You are like water that still flows
>even when you're down.
Your cigarette smoke stinks
>but I do not care
You are like an owl
>full of wisdom
Your sense of humor
>is what makes you whole.
Your toughness is what will keep you alive
>during your sickness.
The one thing I'll never forget
>is the stories you tell
>>up north.

Mike Bradley :: Grade 6
Pine Hill Elementary School :: Cottage Grove

Love Poem

We need love.
It flows around us
In us
Through us
Like a fluid
Yet we cannot touch it

We absorb love
We soak it up
It makes the room thick with Seraphim
It makes us cry
It flows around us
Yet we cannot touch it

Ryan Rasmussen :: Grade 5
Eisenhower Elementary School :: Hopkins

Around the Fire Ring

I want to hear about Aunt Elizabeth
feeding me apricots by the river in summer.
It was the year I spent in the red wagon
endless trips up and down the block
pulled by my slaves. That summer
I was queen and hardly left my four-wheeled throne.
Tell me about that one.

Or tell me about Grandpa's mother
walking through a small Chinese village
at night, four kids in tow.
"We'll go this way," she decided,
left the guide who was making
wide circles with the torch and heading
off into nowhere. "After all," she said.
"A straight line is the shortest distance between two points."
Her straight line led them into a flooded rice paddy
and their shoes sloshed for miles.

But don't remind me of peppermint
sideways dreams
lilacs and pink satin casket linings,
eyes shut and painted colors they never wore.

I want to hear a new story.
We can write it ourselves. Let's name the stars
and watch them chase each other till morning.

Rachel Beck :: Grade 11
Stillwater High School :: Stillwater

The Hand That Unfolded Me

I'm a piece of paper and
you unfolded me.
Now I can see you
and the birds
and the rain.
Now I can see,
and let people read
white words on my inside,
and color pretty pictures on me.
Now you can paint your hand
and stamp it on me
and hang me on a Christmas tree.
You can show me your presents,
then put me in your bed
to sleep with you.
Now I will see everything,
not just the dark.
Thanks, bud.

Nicholas Crisp :: Grade 4
Kennedy Elementary School :: Hastings

Untitled

Down deep, below the inconsequential friendships,
Below the meanings of all those lives,
Lies something very special.
Someone so close, they could be part of
My extraordinarily vivid imagination.
Someone who knows my words before I speak them,
My thoughts before I write them down.
A person who has a certain something that
Connects our minds,
So we think as one entity,
Though living as two.
The worn, dank black combat boots smell, a burnt, shrunk leather
    jacket,
The hysterical fits of laughter
At an extraordinary prank, or inside joke.
These are the memories I have,
And continue to add to my precious
Collection of images of my best friend.

Jason Bistodeau :: Grade 12
Elk River High School :: Elk River

The Love Story

When we are in love,
we love the sound of
the rain hitting the ground—
tip-tap, the mist starting
to clear, the fog opening
up to a bright sunny day.

Travis Morrison :: Grade 3
Gordon Bailey Elementary School :: Woodbury

A Great Person

Theresa Goetzke was born on March 22, 1962, in San Bernadino, California. She has four sisters, a mom, and a dad. She's allergic to cats and smoke. A few things that make her happy are seeing the sun, reading a good book, knowing her kids are happy, and going on walks. A few things that make her unhappy are wars, crimes, crimes against children and suffering.

If she could travel anywhere she would go to Hawaii. She describes herself as a caring, loving and a fun person. I would describe her as a loving, caring, hard worker, good cook, friendly, good listener and the BEST Mom in the World.

Amber Goetzke :: Grade 4
Weaver Elementary School :: Maplewood

My Friend Justin

    I have decided to do my sketch on my friend to the end, Justin McDonough. There are lots of things that most people don't know about him. He was born March 5th, 1983 in St. Paul, Minnesota. Today happens to be March 5, 1993, so he turned ten years old today. He lives here in Maplewood, Minnesota.

    My good friend is an only child and has no pets. He likes baseball, basketball and football. This funny man is in Mrs. Oliver's class at Weaver Elementary School. When he grows up he would like to be a policeman. Like most fourth grade boys, Justin likes rap and Nintendo. He is very funny and very nice. I think you would like him too.

Jesse Bewley :: Grade 4
Weaver Elementary School :: Maplewood

The Captive

The name in this story has been changed to protect the guilty.

"Communism," she screams, thinking a moment then adding, "It's just like we're living in a communist country. If we don't do what they want us to do when and how they want us to they lock us up some place away from the rest of the world. Like Siberia or something."

Allow me to introduce my twin sister Samantha, "Defender of her own justice."

I've listened to her for two hours now. Like a preacher raising and dropping her voice to emphasize the parts of her speech that she especially likes.

She's upset because she had her boyfriend stay longer than he was supposed to and now she is grounded.

We've been sitting in my room on the bed. The conversation (well, if one could call it that) has been entirely one-sided. It's as though I've been watching a t.v. I can't shut off. I don't mind listening to her for about an hour or so but after that I begin to feel as though this is what hell must be like.

It's a good thing God gave me a lot of patience because he also gave me a sister who would send a saint insane.

I sit very still and quiet for two reasons: One, I don't want to do something that would motion to her that I'm sick of the conversation because that would offend her and I don't know which is the worst of the two evils, offending her or listening to her. It's a pretty close call and I figure since I've already survived through half of this there's no need to turn it around and start her on a fresh course of action. Two, like the chameleon I hope to remain still enough to blend into my surroundings and in time be passed up by my predator. And so for the time being sit here a prisoner to the woes of her "miserable existence," as she might tell you.

Don't get me wrong. I love Sam to death. She's my best friend and most of the time I enjoy her company. She is quite amusing when she wants to be. I'm just warning you, that any signs of a "pity party" should be taken seriously because once on a roll she's a skipping record that has to wear itself out before you can stop listening. Let's just say beating dead horses is her specialty.

"Who are our parents, Hitler and Stalin reincarnated?" She whimpers for a bit then says in a hopeless tone, "I'm trapped."

Of course I'm thinking, "So am I. Sam, you're a psychiatrist's nightmare."

I truly don't believe a word Sam says about being trapped though; she's the Houdini of grounded occupants of our house. She may get grounded but she doesn't stay there for long. The last time she was grounded for a week my parents only held out for four days before they lifted her sentence. I suppose the crying, wailing and door slamming just got to them. They began to twitch and blink a lot. When Sam gets grounded it becomes a little confusing as to who is being punished, us or her. Once my parents weigh the evidence they usually rule in our favor and send Sam out of the house.

She has sprawled herself out on my bed like a dying character out of "Hamlet." She is quiet for now. I suppose her mouth is just dry. She'll have to work up some saliva before she starts in again.

I figure if worst comes to worst and she begins her nightmare of woe once again I will have no other choice but to fall off of the side of the bed and act as though I've been injured. That will take care of today which only leaves me with six more days of her or should I say our sentence.

Teresa March :: Grade 12
Long Prairie High School :: Long Prairie

Group Play

Scene: A line of 6 people stand on the edge of the stage. Music plays, drums and other percussion. Music stops. They randomly shout these lines:

STORM ONE: I'm going to blow your house apart.

STORM TWO: You have to stick together. You're a family. I am the fear that can tear you apart. I'm here to show you how much you need each other.

STORM THREE: I will shatter your strength, house. I will defeat you.

STORM FOUR: You are a little thing. I could tear you apart in a second, if I had hands. SHOW YOUR FEAR. SHOW YOUR FEAR.

> The 6 people exit, except for one, who circles the DAD, and says to him:

STORM: SHOW YOUR FEAR. SHOW YOUR FEAR.

EVERYONE: SHOW YOUR FEAR. SHOW YOUR FEAR.

> The last "Storm" voice exits, joins the percussion group. Music builds and diminishes under the next lines:

Scene: Basement of a house. The storm, now only music without the voices, rages outside. The family huddles in silence.

DAD: Looks like it's not getting any better.

MOM: Looks like it's getting worse.

SISTER: What's going to happen to us? What's going to happen to us? What's going to happen to us? What's going to happen to us?

BROTHER: Why can't we go outside?

SISTER: Because idiot. You know why.

> Music builds very loud. DAD cuts it off with a scream.

DAD: QUIET!!!

    Silence.

DAD: EVERYTHING WILL BE OKAAAAAAYYYY. DON'T WORRYYYYY!!!

SON: Ha ha ha.

MOM: I'm hungry. Can't we go upstairs and get some food?

DAD: All right, we'll go get some food but stick together so no one gets hurt.

SISTER: I'll go first.

MOM: (Shouts) NO YOU WON'T. Let your father.

SON: Ha ha ha.

DAD: QUIET!!!

    Silence.

DAD: Hey listen. The walls are beginning to come loose.

    MOM runs around and around.

MOM: Don't Panic! Don't Panic! Don't Panic! Don't Panic! Don't Panic! Don't Panic!

SISTER: I'm not sure I believe you.

    She says this to the DAD as well.

SISTER: I'm not sure I believe you.

    She slowly leaves the house, goes out into the storm. They speak directly to her.

STORM ONE: I'm going to blow your house apart.

STORM TWO: You have to stick together. You're a family. I am the fear that can tear you apart. I'm here to show you how much you need each other.

STORM THREE: I will shatter your strength. I will defeat you.

STORM FOUR: You are a little thing. I could tear you apart in a second, if I had hands. SHOW YOUR FEAR. SHOW YOUR FEAR.

    She looks into the storm. End.

Al Tripp's Class :: *Grade 8*
Rush City Schools :: *Rush City*

So I Tell You Right Now, Good-bye

Untitled

Hollow is a sad place
Black like darkness
A place that is there for thousands of years
It feels lonesome
Echoes like emptiness
Like there is no way out
A place where you are never thought of by another person
Like a baby who has no feelings
Like a baby that doesn't cry
A scary place

Javon Jackson :: Grade 5
Parkway Elementary School :: St. Paul

Your Death

The stars watch us with ice in their eyes.
I search for you
As the wind lifts my hair and stirs my
    blood like the water under the river's ice.
My hands are burning cold
And the black pines have eaten you
    alive.
You are lost, like the sparrow I found
    in the drift.
The moon sees all
So I ask her where you are
But she will not answer.
She wraps herself in a cloud—
a grey shroud.

Becky Raasch :: Grade 12
Willmar High School :: Willmar

I Never Knew I Loved . . .

I never knew I loved
the cool, light breeze of fall
tingling down my spine.

I never knew I loved waiting
for my dad to come home
and give me a big hug,
and whispering "I love you"
softly in my ear.

I never knew I loved the country,
the sound of crickets at night,
splashing in puddles, going on
nature hunts through woods
next to the lot I lived on.

I never knew I loved
sharing my deepest feelings,
waking early on Sundays
to hear about God,
and having Gospel music
drift smoothly into my soul.

But most of all,
I never knew I loved
sharing love, in a family of five,
until I had to get used to love,
in a family of four.

Jessica DeYoung :: Grade 7
Hidden Oaks Middle School :: Prior Lake

Arvelia

Hello Baby Veya
she would say to me
sitting in the hospital
rocking me. Hands shaking
not stopping. Not being able
to hold anything else but me.
She would talk to me, say hello
Baby Veya. How was your day?
She would sing to me.
All I can remember is her
lightish brown eyes and
long black and grey silky hair.
Every morning she would say
hello baby Veya. She always
looked at me. She had a
picture of me on her door.
Then one day she said
good-bye Baby Veya.

Landis-Arvelia Harwell :: Grade 5
Parkway Elementary School :: St. Paul

Old Arizona

I miss
the cattle ranchers,
Dad and I riding horses,
horse races with friends,
silently changing lizards,
tall cactuses,
White Thunder, my horse,
running like the wind.
Arizona gone
like the birds going south.

Earl Tourville :: Grade 5
Royal Oaks Elementary School :: Woodbury

Moving

Dad Transferred.
Horrible.
Boxes everywhere.
Clothes, Toys and Books all going in boxes.
Linens, Pots & Pans all going in boxes.
Moving van here.
Dressers, Bikes and Beds all going in the moving van.
House empty.
Sounds hollow.
Walk through living room.
Go to see my room.
Empty.
Crying.
Friends in yard
Opening and closing their palms and fingers.
It will never be the same.

Beth Williams :: Grade 5
Glen Lake Elementary School :: Hopkins

Untitled

I could feel a hole
when the policeman knocked on my door.
The hole grew
on the ride to the hospital.
The hole growing
and reminding me
I'd never hear his voice again
or smell his apple-scented pipe.
When I saw his gray face,
I wanted to tell him to get up.
That night
when I lay beside my hole,
I prayed it was a dream.
My prayer didn't work.
Now more and more memories
fill the blackness.
Some day the hole will go away,
I hope.

James Adamiak :: Grade 8
Oltman Junior High School :: St. Paul Park

Untitled

I wish I could tell this person's name.
I wish I could tell how he is so strong
but gentle.
I wish I could tell how he wishes he
could hear the wind whistling,
the waves crashing and my voice of gold.
I wish I could tell how he filled my
life with happiness and how I loved
him so much.
I wish I could tell how he broke
my heart.
I wish I could tell how he rolled my
heart over like a steam roller.
I wish I could tell how I don't love him
anymore.
I wish I could tell him his face
is ten thousand worms.
I wish I could . . .

Sarah Connelly :: Grade 6
Plymouth Creek Elementary :: Plymouth

Anxious

Anxious turns colors
Anxious is when someone is wondering, when you're excited or
    curious or nervous
Is when my mom is pregnant
Anxious looks like breaking glass
Anxious looks like a person standing still
Looks like I'm choking
My eyes pop out
I blink my eyes fast
I sweat and my feet move
My brain ticks
Body gets hard, gives hope, wiggles
I will talk little by little
I get hungry
Anxious is scared when someone breaks in my house and steals

Lolly Pederson's Class :: Grade 4
Parkway Elementary School :: St. Paul

What a Tangled Web We Weave

I dance through your black veils,
deception, temptation, a burning love.
Intoxicated, moving from one to another,
blindly seeing my way.

Twirling, tossed upon the seas of right
and wrong.
Hurting, as I pass through these silky veils,
never finding the end of this rich fabric,
never moving forward.

Only one way to go, backwards.
I retrace my steps, backing carefully away
from the spider's web, enchanted, still,
yet seeing the beginning near, and now,
very clearly.
I crawl to the opening, shedding the veils
that still cling to my arms.
A healing takes place.
No more looking back.

Becky Weets :: Grade 11
KMS High School :: Kerkhoven

To My Uncle Carl

I felt like an open door,
    with you, the wind,
        passing through me
            without me noticing.

I didn't realize
    I would never
        feel your wind again.

If I'd known
    I would have closed my door
        and said Good-bye.

So I tell you
    right now,
        Good-bye.

Joel Wertheim :: Grade 5
Meadowbrook Elementary School :: Hopkins

Forever Wasn't Enough

The sun
set high in the blue,
a warm summer day,
but inside me dark,
full of sorrow.
The wind and the sight of children playing
whirring past us in a blur.
We didn't want to
but we had to.
Those dark unknowing eyes
stared through my heart.
I couldn't look,
couldn't bear it.
Warm tears welled.
We had to.
The soft fuzzy fur,
his body warm against mine.
Never wanting to let go.
Memories flooded my mind as
the world whirred past in a blur.
The drive took forever,
but for me forever wasn't enough.
So small, not knowing what would happen
that warm summer day.
We didn't want to.
We had to.

Pacho Lara :: Grade 8
Central Middle School :: Columbia Heights

Why Did God Pick Me?

I never knew I could feel such fear
until I heard the door open
and I walked up the stairs
and saw you standing there.
I never knew I could feel such fear
until you started choking the children
and you started to talk about respecting
and doing what adults tell you.
I never knew I could feel such fear
until you started to talk
about how everyone should believe in Satan
and you told the children it was time for them to go to bed
because we were going to do something they shouldn't see
I never knew I could feel such fear
until you looked at me
with a funny smirk on your face
and you went upstairs to put the children to bed
and I ran to the phone.
I never knew I could feel such fear
until my dad came
I was crying
and ran in my dad's arms
and I told him there was a man in the bedroom.
I never knew I could feel such fear
until my father told him to leave
and my dad, the children and I came back
and you had kicked in the door.
I never knew I could feel such fear
until I saw your car getting pulled away
and the police said
you would be out in a few days.
I never knew I could feel such fear
until I closed my eyes
all I could see was you.
I never knew I could feel such fear

from a single human being.
I never knew!
I never knew!
I never knew!

Terra Pehl :: Grade 8
Mahtomedi Middle School :: Mahtomedi

The Dream is Over

Adrenalin.
The beat getting stronger and
                         stronger
pace slowly to position
psyched   pumped up
    ready to go
the music begins
the dance starts to flow
       and like fireworks
    spurting into the air
tossing and turning
    bam!
       I stuck the landing
    injected with more energy
loving it—music even louder
    dancing your heart out
       putting your all into
  your dreams
    unbeatable
       suddenly   an explosion
    the first foot lands
Pain   it hurts
    what's happening
I can't move it, my leg,
    Help me   She's injured
I heard
    my heart sank.
It's all over.

Maggie McCormack :: Grade 9
Willmar Junior High School :: Willmar

KATIE

Emerald eyes sparkled with curiosity,
cheeks rosy with excitement,
lips curved up in charming smile,
voice jolly with life,
chocolate brown hair flowing down her back,
her inside burst with love and laughter.

Then one day,
her eyes were now a dull green,
face pale as a new layer of snow,
her smile fighting to come out,
voice hoarse,
hair lost from chemotherapy;
but her inside never changed—
she lifted us with her uplifting thoughts.

Katie died in her mother's arms,
and even though I wasn't there,
I could feel it happen.
She took a part of each person she knew.
I often see her face in my dreams,
looking down from the heavens.

Stephanie Hickman :: Grade 8
Oltman Junior High School :: St. Paul Park

The News

On the Death of Mike Olson

Punched in the mouth.
What? I say.
But I already heard.
How? I say
Why? I say
He was so young
He can't be gone!
I ask them again
But they just whisper
So sad, so sad.

Dinner is eaten in silence.
I quickly excuse myself
to disappear into my room.
Silence greets me.
I sit,
Think,
I remember.
Outside, the last glimmer
of sunlight disappears
But I don't turn on a light.

Peter Majerle :: Grade 8
Central Middle School :: Columbia Heights

The White Van

Every time I see a white van
I remember my friend,
I knew she would go,
Just not so soon.

I ran outside to say good-bye.
I remember the wind
Slapping my face.
The van blinked its lights,
Impatient.
"Don't go!" I cried.
Too late.

The van pulled out of the driveway.
She leaned out the window,
Calling, "I'll write!"
She hasn't.
Not yet.
I watched the van. Further.
It went away . . . further . . . further . . .
It's gone.

Beth Knudsen :: Grade 5
Heart of the Lakes Elementary School :: Perham

Grandpa "Mac"

The time had come. The time I had been
avoiding all night. I examined the clock,
the minute hand crawling closer and closer
to the immense number 9. It was time.
Everyone was ready, physically anyway.
It was simple for us to walk to the car.
The arctic cold hit me like a pinch to my face.
I stared out the car window, lost in my own world,
unaware of any voices and noises going on around me.
The 20 minute drive seemed to take seconds.
I longed for time to stop, completely end.
I knew this would be the most important trip
of my life so far.
We were there.
I walked like a turtle towards the room.
My mouth tasted dry, like I'd just eaten a gallon
of peanut butter.
I could feel my body vibrating, along with the
thumping pulse in my neck and wiggling knot
in my gut.
The smell was wretched. How could anyone stay here?
"My legs are going to give out. I just know it."
I finally brought myself to trudge into the room.
There he was, sitting like a doll in a chair.
Words blurry, but heart focused, he told me about
the cattle and weather. Small talk.
Here I am talking small talk, avoiding
the issue at hand.
My heart longed to speak, but my voice said,
"It's getting colder out."
It was time to leave,
leave and say good-bye—

"Good-bye and I love you," for the last time.
I stood there like a statue in the doorway—staring.
Knowing I could never look again at him.
My icicle tears stung like bees on my cheeks.
I glanced outside—"Good-bye for the last time."

Nicole Borgert :: Grade 12
Swanville Public School :: Swanville

Untitled

Too much sadness,
thunder too loud,
weather is shy.
The cry is too heavy,
drops so light,
wet hearts,
relaxing trees,
rain.

Jan Gitter :: Grade 7
GFW Middle School :: Fairfax

Tribels

Tribels was very poor. She was a barn cat and her owner was poor, too, so he had no money to feed her. One day her owner was talking on the phone. Tribels wondered who it was. The next day she was taken in a cage made of wood. The owner said he was sorry, for he was poor. That night she was taken to a shelter where she could eat and be poor no more.

Devin M. Tkachuck :: Grade 3
Mounds Park All Nations School :: St. Paul

Where Magic Can Secretly Happen

James and Desire

I love to not just listen
but to hear him play,
flowing
his emotions through
the strings, his moods
amazing
sometimes he sings
when he doesn't
better; I can lyric
my own
hours I could
be mesmerized.
I wish

I had an emotion-
outletting art—
the mind of
M.C. Escher, ee cummings
a cluttered
pulsating, productive
fishbowl atop my shoulders
with uniques and creatives
swimming around
and around

then
I in circles to myself
could talk
and people alone would leave
me but
lonely I wouldn't be
cuz I'd love my it
my spesheealitie
keep it on an elastic leash,
and teach it tricks
Daydream
I'd name it.

Angela K. Johnson :: Grade 12
Battle Lake High School :: Battle Lake

The Giant Step to Cambodia

I fell asleep. I crossed the Pacific with one big giant step to Cambodia. I saw the big trees, and I saw a house with my great-grandmother and father. He looked like a very wise man, and he was. He took something out of his pockets. He put it in a bowl. He took water and put it in. Then he put it over the fire. He said Taste it. It tasted so good I had five bowls.

I smelled the trees. We went outside and danced in the rain. It felt like a cold shower. After that, we dried out with leaves and the sun came up. We went to town, where my great-grandmother owned a store. She made blankets. They were beautiful. She gave me one. It was the coolest blanket I ever saw. I went back to America just when I woke up.

Sothara Has :: Grade 4
Chelsea Heights Elementary School :: St. Paul

Imagination

Imagination floats in the air at night,
making your dreams fly.
In daytime, it wanders
like a lonely traveler that's lost.
When you sit,
doing nothing at all,
it floats up in the clouds
to the sky.
It dances on clouds, floats in the air,
and takes rides on an angel's wings.
It flies, flies, flies.

When you move with a start,
your imagination flies back to earth
and lands back where it belongs.

Bernadette Murphy :: Grade 4
Pullman Elementary School :: St. Paul Park

ODE TO LACES

On my toe shoes, pink laces flow
like an ocean's rippling waves.
On my toe shoes they wrap around my
ankles like snakes, when I tie them
in a bow it is like rabbit ears
popping from inside a hole.
They ripple like chocolate fudge rolling
down vanilla ice cream, waiting
to be eaten.
A little balloon floating through
the sky, unowned, that's my laces.
Hanging on a wall they are streaks
of flowing hair on a gorgeous princess.
And when I dance with them
they make me float on the ocean of air.

Dena Gruber :: Grade 5
Birch Grove Elementary School :: Brooklyn Park

Excerpt from The Heaven Land Book

I'm in Heaven Land. I meet my friends Linda and Mary. We wash our feet. We like it here because the cloud is soft. We talk a lot. Linda said she likes it here. And Mary said she doesn't like it here.

Linda, Mary and I are looking for three wands, and the colors are peach, blue-green and red. Then we come to the dark place and we see three wands.

Then the wind blows and we can't get the wands so we fly up in the sky. Then the wind stops blowing. Then the three of us fly down and get the wands.

And the wands turn all the things to heart—heart chair, heart light. We live there forever.

Yen Dang :: Grade 2
Parkway Elementary School :: St. Paul

A Crazy Poem to Read

My poem is a toddler who walks around
in a daze.
I want to climb out the window
and run wild.
I want to swim my way to Neptune.
I will annoy my teacher with the
beeper on my new watch.
I want to jinx all who like war.
Ah, but my poem,
My poem can feel the breath of a dead
person.
My poem is stronger than liquid Tide with
color guard.
My poem can fly to the top of the world
and turn polka dots into swans.
My poem can reach the unreachable,
My poem can do what man can't,
But together, not only my poem is
strong, but I am too.

Mary Beth D'Agosta :: Grade 5
Katherine Curren Elementary School :: Hopkins

Mountain Secret, Mind Fire

In the meadow
through the mountains
to my secret place,

The place where no one goes,
where the wind blows,
blows so fine.

In my mind house
with a warm leaf bed,
by my mind fire
that burns so well,

This is where
my imagination grows,
and unlocks the mind world,
where magic can secretly happen.

Anna Williams :: Grade 4
Richfield Intermediate School :: Richfield

Good Night, My Puppy

Good night Coco
Good night puppy
I hope you have sweet
dreams. I'll come and
brush your teeth for you.
The fireflies are out.
You don't know how to
brush your teeth, so I
will do it for you. Good
night. Sleep tight.
Shhhhhh . . .

Natalie Homa :: Grade 2
Webster Magnet School :: St. Paul

Elisa's Dreams
(from The Seven Swans)

I mourn day and night for the
white feathers on my brother's arm.

Forgiveness is unreachable.

Like a cripple he wanders castle
halls.

Footsteps constant, ever searching.
dreams of valor, unrequited

Love, a maiden's cool hands
shall never hold this

sorry winged creature.

Not bird, not man, he cannot fly
from this wakened nightmare.

In dreams I knit,
golden gossamer stitches
cover white doves.

The feathers are eternal.

Jennifer Workman :: Grade 5
Middleton Elementary School :: Woodbury

Five Minutes of Exercise

I am a filter,
a filter for music.
I sense the rhythmic waves.
I open my mind
letting in only those waves.
I sit on my amp
and pick up my bass
letting four strings talk.
They speak in deep tones
going out of my amp
and into the air.
I sense the vibration
around me.
In my mind
I imagine the notes going
in a smooth field-like pattern,
going a thumpy rhythm
and repeating.
The music controls me.
I am like a robot—
fingers no longer
going at free will.
The music moves like waterfall
staying in a steady complex rhythm.
At last the pain in my fingers
is too great.
I can no longer play.
I turn off my amp.
The sound waits for me in the air.

Liam McNally :: Grade 7
Oltman Junior High School :: St. Paul Park

Gotta Write!

Gotta write about friends
Gotta write about children
Gotta write about people
Just listen to me
Gotta write about animals
Gotta write about peaches
Sing a song, listen to the beat

Gotta write about the earth
Gotta write about airplanes
Gotta write about old songs
Just listen to me
Gotta write about flowers
Gotta write about horses
Sing a song, listen to the beat

    Listen to the beat, you and me
    Listen to the beat, you and me
    Sing a song, listen to the beat
    Listen to the beat, you and me
    Listen to the beat, you and me
    Sing a song, listen to the beat

Gotta write about zebras
Gotta write about the world
Gotta write about love
Just listen to me
Gotta write about monkeys
Gotta write about toothbrushes
Sing a song, listen to the beat

Gotta write about Elvis
Gotta write about gerbils
Gotta write about snakes
Just listen to me
Gotta write about parakeets
Gotta write about baboons
Sing a song, listen to the beat

Robert Axberg's Class :: MMH
Parkway Elementary School :: St. Paul

COME HOME BEFORE DARK

Free Spirit

I am the eagle that soars
through the clear bright sky,
the bear fishing on a warm
spring day.

I am the baby deer who has
no worries.
I am the Indian warrior out
on the Montana plains of life,
the one single white buffalo.

I am the Free Spirit that
everyone needs.

I am the stars mother earth shot
from her breast,
the light from brother moon.
I am the raccoon who drinks
from water's edge,
the black mustang running
wild in the wind.

Shannon Nibbe :: Grade 12
Alternative Learning Center :: St. Paul Park

Old Woman

Old woman with
rocking chair a
very serious face, belt
that comes up to her
chest wrinkly face.
Across the street of
houses thinking of
a mansion in the
country, my house
behind me, this is my
dying wish. Sun half
on the house in the shade
All I need is air, getting
cold, long white dress
cannot see my high button
shoes.

Deon Klein :: Grade 5
Parkway Elementary School :: St. Paul

The Desk

The Desk is a Kangaroo
sticking its baby in its pocket
to keep it from falling on the floor
where the hungry lion waits.
The desk is a Kangaroo jumping, eating grass,
playing games with the baby to teach it
how to jump. The desk is a Kangaroo
that boxes with its feet,
that uses its tail for a chair,
that never learned how to swim.

II
Now the desk is a turtle
scared into its shell. Now
the desk is a turtle biting your finger.
Now it is swimming like taking a shower
in the water. Now it's jumping rope,
now it's hiding, now sleeping.
All night the desks open their mouths
like dinosaurs under the moon and stars.
All night they cry because they have no
girl friends, and boy friends are as boring
as clams. All night they cry
under the stars, all night,
with tears like diamonds.

Margaret Mogck's Class :: TESOL
North End Elementary School :: St. Paul

To My Guitar

You have become like a puppy to me.
Almost as a baby is to his mother.
Your face shines like the sun.
You sing to me.

You are mine to hold and caress.
My fingers dance happily on your long, slender neck.
Another day they pound you.
They may threaten to break you,
Pull your hair out,
But you are patient.

You laugh for me,
    Cry for me,
        Shout for me,
Whisper for me.
Like a continuous, ever-burning candle,
    Always there for me to find myself.

I will give you a special place,
    Your own bed.
When I leave you my fingers will not forget you.

I will listen to your brothers and sisters,
Singing.
They all translate a language
Deeper than the obvious.
    As you do for me,
        My Guitar.

Josh LaFond :: Grade 11
Perham High School :: Perham

The Horse

If the horse
comes by my window
I will start
to grow
a mane so white
I will start
to grow a tail
and I will get
four hooves
I will get short white hairs
I will start prancing
around my room
I will go outside
and prance around
in the grass
I will hear
the rustling
of the greenest grass
I will taste
the freshest hay
I will touch the ground
so lightly
I will smell
like I just had a bath
I will see the light that twinkles

Betsy Murphy :: Grade 3
Blue Earth Elementary School :: Blue Earth

I Am

I am the shiny unicorn playing in the colorful rainbow,
I am the sweet cherry everyone loves,
I am the stars that shine at night,
I am the sky that holds the moon, sun, stars and clouds,
I am the fish that rolls through the water,
I am the eagle playing in the sky,
I am the sun that shines on the flowers so they could grow,
I am the bunny who hides the eggs on Easter,
I am the water splashing swish swash,
I am the blue horse running through the meadow,
I am the wind carrying light things through the air.

Hnou Moua :: Grade 2
Parkway Elementary School :: St. Paul

Let the Storms Come

Poets are gods of language,
with lightning bolt imaginations
and thunderous vocabulary,
they start storms.

Storms of feeling,
each individual has
and should share.

When the sun comes out,
the grass begins to grow
just like new ideas.
The storm starts all over again.
Let the storms come.

Kyle Swanson :: Grade 7
Oltman Junior High School :: St. Paul Park

Untitled

My poem is a lion chasing away the night. The tornado of my poem tears up the ground. The river of my poem washes through the valley. My poem is a nut tree with nice big nuts. My poem is a secret that cannot disappear.

Henry Mundstock :: Grade 2
Pilot Knob Elementary School :: Eagan

Arnold the Alligator

Once there was an alligator who lived in a swamp. He had two brothers and four sisters. He hated to live in the swamp. He wanted to live in a fancy indoor pool and he wanted to eat raw fish. One day a movie producer was walking by the swamp. When he saw Arnold, his face lit up like a light bulb. He asked Arnold if he wanted to be in a movie, but he had to leave his family.

When Arnold heard the word "movie" he started to swim around and with a loud voice, he said, "YES!" He asked, "Would I be living in a fancy pool and get to eat raw fish?"

"Certainly."

Arnold was so happy he was standing on the tip of his tail. The movie producer told Arnold that he could move tomorrow.

When he got to the fancy pool, he jumped in right away. But there was a big problem. They wanted to paint Arnold's tail orange! Right away in a louder voice than at the swamp, he said, "No!"

Then they asked, "If you don't like orange, I can stick with purple."

But Arnold still said, "No!" Then Arnold said, "If you won't let me be green, I will not be in the movie."

Then the movie guy asked, "How about we put on an orange alligator costume?"

Arnold said that he would have to think about it, and that he would tell him tomorrow morning.

When morning came Arnold said that he would. The movie guy said that they would start practicing at noon that day. Then the movie guy went out to buy the costume. When he got back they tried the costume on for size. The tail was a little long, but it fit perfectly otherwise. When it was time to start filming the movie, Arnold was so excited that when he was done practicing his lines and it was time for the movie to start he forgot his lines. So they went over his lines with him again.

It sure was a good thing that the movie producer was patient or Arnold would have been fired.

The movie was about two alligators who hated each other, but at the end of the story they became best friends. The next day Arnold had to get up at about 5 a.m. to film the movie. Then the movie producer gave Arnold a schedule for when he had to get up every morning.

When he had been filming for two weeks he was really getting tired of getting up at the times the movie producer assigned. He especially hated getting up on Mondays. So he had to talk to the movie producer.

Arnold said, "I am getting too tired even when I have weekends off, so I quit."

Arnold learned that you can't be what you're not. He moved out that night back into the swamp and he never wanted to be in a movie ever again!

Shannon Rawson :: Grade 4
Mounds Park All Nations School :: St. Paul

Group Play

Based on a dream by Julie Hatler, created by the class.

Scene: The kitchen. MOM and the GIRL are baking cookies. Two flutes play a haunting, pulsing sound.

MOM: (smiling) I hope the cookies turned out all right.

(She takes cookies from the oven. She looks at them, and her face grows angry. Flutes stop, and a sound of shaking, like maracas or a rattle snake, comes in. MOM slams the cookie sheet onto the counter next to the GIRL.)

MOM: WHAT DID YOU DO?!!

GIRL: (Sheepishly) I guess I put the wrong ingredient in.

MOM: HOW COULD YOU DO THAT?

(She steps forward, raises her arms up, shouts, along with the sound of the flutes playing high notes, piercing, like a siren:)

MOM: Ronnnnnnnnn!!!

(RON, the dad enters, carrying a chair. With a strong drumbeat he walks slowly towards the GIRL.)

RON: Don't worry dear, here I come.

(He gets to the GIRL, raises the chair and puts it on her head.)

GIRL: Nooooooo!!

(RON pushes the chair downwards, pressing the GIRL to the floor, with the chair on top of her. Saxophones play wild erratic notes during this. Saxophones stop. RON sits on the chair with the GIRL under it. He lifts his leg, and farts with a huge blatt from the saxophone. MOM cheers and laughs. He does it again louder. One more time, louder. RON and MOM dance around the GIRL under the chair as wild music plays: drum, sax, rattle and flutes. They cheer and laugh and point at the GIRL. Then they stand and look at her. The wild music stops, and the flutes play again, the same haunting, pulsing music from the beginning, before the problem started. They look at her for a long time, until the laughter from the audience goes away, and the mood comes way down, to sadness. Then:)

MOM: Look what we've done to her.

(RON wanders off, zig zagging aimlessly, as if lost.)

RON: What do I say? What do I say? What do I say? What do I say?

(He exits. MOM looks at the GIRL a long time. She takes the chair off her. She looks. She starts off in the direction of RON. She gets to the door.)

GIRL: Mom?

(MOM stops. Does not look at the GIRL.)

MOM: Yes?

GIRL: Can you help me?

(MOM waits. She exits through the door. There is a long pause. We become convinced that the parents have abandoned the GIRL. Then the door opens, and MOM and RON enter. They go to the GIRL, and sit next to her.)

End of the play.

Chris Collin's Class :: Grade 6
Hillside Elementary School :: Cottage Grove

Half Man Half Woman

Once upon a time there was a man and a woman who were stuck together. They were married. Their names were Bill and Beth. These two hated to be stuck together. Bill didn't like Beth watching him eat or doing his work. Beth said, "Well, that's your problem, because I didn't make us be stuck together." Then she started to cry. But, you see whenever Beth cries Bill has to cry too, because they both have just one of the eyes. One day Bill said to Beth, "Beth I have to go to the bathroom." She said, "Fine" and closed her eye. Then they switched it around and they were done with that day's duty. At about 3:00 in the afternoon, Bill wanted to go for the walk that they were supposed to take at 8:00. Beth wanted to take her 3:00 nap. They sat there and argued until 9:00 and so Beth got her way, because it was time for them to go to sleep. Three years later they were living happily with five kids: Dan, Mitch, Linda, Jesse, and of course Heidi. One day they got really mad at each other and Bill wanted a divorce and he wanted to keep: Linda, Jesse and Mitch. Beth got Heidi and Dan. There was only one problem—they were stuck together, so Dan went and got the chainsaw and split them in half. right then they went and got another person's half body and lived miserably ever after, because they missed each other so bad, it hurt!!!!!!!!!!!!!!!!!!!!!!!!!!

Jamie Miller :: Grade 5
Parkway Elementary School :: St. Paul

My Place in the World

The Soft Side of Me

I am a friend to the subtle sun at dawn
scattering warm soft colors over the sky
like a painter's brush
tingling my nerves
starting them for the day that lies ahead.

I am a friend to the small squirrels
that depend on myself and my family
for nourishment during the winter.
They come to me
to my hand
not hesitating
trusting
not afraid.

I am a friend to the wind
the breeze that holds me from toppling over in spring.
In my own way
the wind carries me up and over the world
not dropping me
the soft side of me.

Ashley Thomas Kjos :: Grade 5
Oakridge Elementary School :: Eagan

Nature

Why is the sky blue?
It reflects the colors of the lakes.

Why do the stars twinkle?
They are winking at the moon.

How does the wind blow?
The trees whip it into shape.

Why is the snow white?
It is slivers of clouds playing
freeze tag.

What makes a seed grow?
The sun is convincing life to
come out of the earth.

How does a bird know where to migrate?
They follow the highways that bring
their hearts home.

Heidi McKay :: Grade 6
Barnum Elementary School :: Barnum

How Lizard Changed Color

Once Lizard could not change color.
Back then, all colors were trapped in Rock.
One day, another animal chased Lizard.
Lizard fell into Rock. He fell into sleep.
When Lizard woke up, whatever he was on,
he would camouflage with.
The colors in Rock were not there anymore.
Lizard took the colors into him.
Now Rock is gray.

Kelly Crandall :: Grade 2
Lakeview Elementary School :: Robbinsdale

Bear

Bear looks around.
He sees trees and light coming through the clouds.
Bear notices the flash of a bird moving from one tree
to another.
Bear hears the sound of wolves howling
at the remaining stars.
He is shocked by the sound of
frogs in the near pond.

I used to imagine the frightful look
in Bear's eyes,
the freedom he felt and the smell
of the fresh air, pine cones in the
morning mist.
He touches the chilling sunrise wind,
and the cold air going through his
mouth while he breathes.
I used to imagine Bear going
for a walk
tasting the berries of the bushes
that surround his home.

Kelly Michels :: Grade 7
LeSueur/Henderson Junior/Senior High School :: LeSueur

Praise to Nature

Praise to the ocean
for it supplies life on earth.

Praise to the bear
whose soul is like a valley covered
in fog.

Praise to the weeping willow
who brings us shade like a
sad shadow.

Praise to the streams for they
wash away our pain.

Praise to the evening for it gives
us something relaxing to look at.

At last, Praise to the wind for
it brushes over our earth and
cleans us and also earth.

Dustin Rosel :: Grade 7
Southland Middle School :: Elkton

SUN	BLUE
The ground looks	like the sound the sky makes
hot as water	when it's full of wind
that took out fire	and thunder.
The playground	Blue saltwater,
is yellow with bananas,	whales jumping
with trees. Be careful	going back in,
don't trip on the bananas	gentian, lilac, hydrangea
or you might splatter	in the heavy world-spreading
	scent of blue
Sunlight will turn the whole world	blue, blue, like blue-jays
	will give
yellow. You will have to	sing everything blue,
swim home in the sunlight.	and be sticky as Kool-Aid.

Ann Reidell's Class :: Grade 1
Parkway Elementary School :: St. Paul

ORANGUTANS

We are the orangutans. We live in the rain forests of Sumatra and Borneo. The danger we are in consists of only one predator and that is the human race. We try to stick to our own lives but the human race interferes. We are shy and inoffensive, which makes us easy to kill and capture. Humans are cutting down our forest homes, which makes us vulnerable. We love to live in family groups. We are geographically separated from our relatives and ancestors, who live in Africa. We all think that our bodies look better in the wild rather than behind bars. Stop killing us.

Heather Tichy, Jacob Richards,
Jeff Sellman and Tara Stuntebec :: Grade 6
Wadena-Deer Creek Elementary School :: Deer Creek

DO YOU KNOW?*

Do you know what the world will be like when you're gone?
Will the grass be green, or yellow?
Will the breeze still rustle in the trees?
Will the water be clean?
Do you know? Do you know?

Do you know what the world will be like when you're gone?
Will the sky be blue or grey?
Will there be food for the animals?
Will there be flowers for the bees?
Do you know? Do you know?

Do you know what the world will be like when you're gone?
Will there be food for everyone?
Will the sun shine down on the people below?
Do you know, do you know?

Do you know what the world will be like when you're gone?
Will the water be clear or cloudy?
Will fish still be in the lakes
And swimming in the sea
Do you know, do you know?

Colleen Hendrick :: Grade 4
Goodview Elementary School :: Winona

*Additional words by Ms. Downie's Grade 4 class, and Ms. Tibor's and Ms. Grob's Grade 2 classes

Do you know what the world will be like when you're gone? Will the grass be green or yellow? Will the breeze still rustle in the trees? Will the water be clean? Do you know? Do you know?

Ladyslipper

We travel the valley between two mountains
End of summer leaves beginning to turn golden
The smell of rain overflowing my senses
Tranquil, peaceful, only the sweet sound of the birds
Water drying up, grass burns easily
The one we journey to see nearby, I can feel it.
Sun low in sky, shadows dance upon the mountains, scary those
    shadows.
The wind blows suddenly, then dies
Almost as quickly as it arose.
An eagle swoops down a high scream of disappointment when her prey
    eludes her.
There the owl in that tree feathers ruffled beak sharp and pointy.
He stares as we approach silently almost cautiously.
The owl's roving eyes perturb us.
We sit quietly waiting for it to speak.
He is finished, we feel tranquil and slip quietly away.
He raises up and sails away.
It was like we had never been there.
We will never forget what he said:
Life is like a woodland ladyslipper slow to bloom.

Anya Scholl :: Grade 8
Worthington Area Junior High School :: Worthington

My Garden

My garden is sprouting.
New carrots help my eyes to see better,
My kiwi is bittersweet.
My lettuce keeps my hungry rabbit alive.
My tomato is juicy and red
(and I can throw it at you).
My apples are sweet
and they will take your loose teeth.
My oranges are squirty
and the inner skin is clear.

Darla Heil's Class :: Grade 3
North End Elementary School :: St. Paul

Just Like Today

Just like today, that old highway

Runs so freely,

Just like today, that old highway runs away. . . . .

        Used to be a pony express
        Travel down a dirt road
        People came in fancy dress
        Or with a heavy load. . . . .

        Blue Earth, Winnebago
        Garden City and Mankato
        Cambridge, Minneapolis
        It will set you free. . . . .

        Pioneers and settlers
        Fur traders and peddlers
        Indians and pilgrims
        All traveled here. . . . .

        It's a place where you can go
        Going fast or going slow
        Its spirit calls us here and there
          It's in your soul, it's in the air. . . . .

Songwriting Group :: Grade 8
Wellcome Memorial Middle School :: Lake Crystal

Chorus
A F♯min D
Just like to - day that old high - way
E7 A F♯min
runs so free - ly, Just like to - day that old
D E7 A
high - way runs a - way.
Verse
A D
Used to be a po - ny ex - press
E7 A
tra - vel down a dirt road.
F♯min D
Peo - ple came in fan - cy dress
B7 E7
or with a hea - vy load.

Arkansas

Arkansas, your winters are as calm
as an old mare. Your summers
are blazing hot, like a fire going
in a fireplace. The spring air
feels like the soft and warm breath
of a horse. The fall
is as gorgeous as a butterfly flying
in the soft wind, when all the leaves
leave their home and hover
over the ground as it falls
into a deep winter's sleep.
The sunsets are as beautiful as
anything I've seen. Now and then I
stop to think and look up into the sky
and see God's wondrous place
and He has created all of this land
and I thank him for this land He created.

Emily Gamble :: Grade 5
Swanville Public Schools :: Swanville

The Black Leopard

The black Leopard is black like midnight
He tastes like shiny black licorice.
He sounds like roaring thunder.
He looks like a black streak of lightning.
He smells like the wind in the trees.
He makes me feel excitedly scared.

Edward Burch, Jr. :: *Grade 3*
Webster Magnet School :: *St. Paul*

I Am

I am the panther
with black furry
skin who leaps through
the dark green jungle.
I am the river with a fast
flowing current with big flowing
bubbles upon the foamy surface.
I am the violet blooming in
the sunshine with big purple
petals in a garden of green.
I am a meteorite shooting
from space like a silver
arrow as rushing air rushes
past.

Kim Oster :: Grade 1
Aquila Primary Center :: St. Louis Park

White

White, something that you've
never seen before

like the white on the caps
that roll on the ocean

like the white sun going
                down
                down
                down

beyond the sea, beyond the moon
and even beyond the stars

white roams where it wants to

in love and in lies, in heaven
and in the land of the dead.

White comes
and white goes

to the peak of the snowiest
mountain to the depth of the
sandiest sea

White is there, everywhere.

        Open your eyes.

Louis Smeby :: Grade 6
Pullman Elementary School :: St. Paul Park

Polished Works of Art

My agates are polished works of art,
each line a person playing
on a hot summer's day.
I once was given an agate
as blue as the open sea.
The lines in it
look like cave drawings
from ancient times.
There are crevices in it
deeper than the deepest hole.
The patterns in the agate are
ocean waves
in the sunset.

Bryan Shattuck :: Grade 6
Chelsea Heights Elementary School :: St. Paul

The Place Where the Forest Doesn't Grow

I am going to the place where the forest doesn't grow.
Where there once was a tree, now there is a stump.
Where bulldozer tracks are everywhere,
the animal bones here and there.
Where the birds no longer sing their sweet song
because now they don't belong.
I am going to the place where the forest doesn't grow,
where the air once was clean, now is dirty
from a power plant that puffs out smoke
all day and night.
Where there once was a meadow where the fox ran around,
now there are malls, and cars and streets,
and hotels, stores, and dirty money and . . .
You know what? I don't think I want to go
to the place where the forest doesn't grow.

Shannon Schulte :: Grade 6
Caledonia Elementary School :: Caledonia

Watching

Sitting high in my tree,
I watch the leaves rustle
Like the waves of crystal clear blue sea.
Watching a flower open
Is like a cloud
Being pushed away
So sun can shine.
Watching grass wave
Is like a bird
Flying gently over sky.
Watching fish swim
Is like a rabbit,
Darting swiftly over land.
Watching a deer look
Is like finding out
A big secret,
The secret of poetry.

Kristi Schneider :: Grade 4
Christa McAuliffe Elementary School :: Hastings

My Cat Felix

I have an alarm clock
covered with fur.

A sandpaper kiss—

that's the way
for a day to begin.

Nicole Kliber :: Grade 5
Lakeview Elementary School :: Robbinsdale

LOVE OF WILDERNESS

Though the forest may be dark
and the animals angry
as they gnash their large teeth,
if you show your love of the wild,
the trees may become
brilliant with light and
the creatures may let their anger
fall away and
look at you through kind eyes
fondling you
as you make your way down the path.
But only if you show
your love of the wilderness.

Cory Gross :: Grade 8
Oltman Junior High School :: St. Paul Park

My Place

I scout around,
no one's there
> so I tip-toe to my secret spot under the old pine tree.

It's quiet,
no one's there
> so I slide down to the basement of my private little world
> and sit, looking up at the baby blue sky.

In my tiny house,
> I crawl to my pretend shed in the basement
> and gather kindling for my pretend fire.

Then I fetch pine cones from underneath the white ocean of snow.
I drag it all back to the top,
> lay it all out
> and toss pine cones into the imaginary fire.

I sit down in my rock chair
> and smell the cool night's air
> and the old pine tree.

I think, I am where no one can see me,
> beneath the matted-down branches of the great pine,
>> and this is my place,
>> my place in the world.

Erin Troutfetter :: Grade 5
Gatewood Elementary School :: Hopkins

Author Index

Andy Acuff	Parkway Elementary School 12
James Adamiak	Oltman Junior High School........................72
Sara Allen	Grand Rapids High School........................35
Diane Arvidson's Class	Parkway Elementary School 9
Robert Axberg's Class	Parkway Elementary School 101
Timmy Babatz	Aquila Primary Center 40
Rachel Beck	Stillwater High School 54
Jesse Bewley	Weaver Elementary School 59
Jason Bistodeau	Elk River High School...............................56
Nicole Borgert	Swanville Public Schools 84
Mike Bradley	Pine Hill Elementary School........................52
Keith Brown	Oltman Junior High School........................46
Edward Burch, Jr.	Webster Magnet School 132
Joe Burns	Pullman Elementary School........................43
Chris Collins' Class	Hillside Elementary School........................114
Lance Collman	Callaway Elementary School 15
Sarah Connelly	Plymouth Creek Elementary School............73
Kelly Crandall	Lakeview Elementary School....................120
Nicholas Crisp	J.F. Kennedy Elementary School 55
Anna Curtis	Blake Middle School 42
Yen Dang	Parkway Elementary School 95
Jessica DeYoung	Hidden Oaks Middle School 68
Courtnie Dornfeld	Chelsea Heights Elementary School...............3
Mary Beth D'Agosta	Katherine Curren Elementary School 96
Sara Ennen	Elm Creek Elementary School....................28
Luther Flagstad	Chelsea Heights Elementary School............44
Emily Gamble	Swanville Public Schools 131
Aisha Ghanchi	Blake Middle School 36
Erica Gilberg	Stillwater Junior High School 14
Jan Gitter	GFW Middle School 86
Amber Goetzke	Weaver Elementary School 58
Amanda Grachek	St. Michael Elementary School 50
Cory Gross	Oltman Junior High School......................139
Dena Gruber	Birch Grove Elementary School 94
Jessica Gruenberg	Aquila Primary Center 24

Kristi Hamlin	Kingsland Elementary School	25
Brian Harms	Prior Lake High School	38
Landis-Arvelia Harwell	Parkway Elementary School	69
Sothara Has	Chelsea Heights Elementary School	92
Greg Hegedus	Alice Smith Elementary School	33
Darla Heil's Class	North End Elementary School	128
Colleen Hendrick	Goodview Elementary School	125
Stephanie Hickman	Oltman Junior High School	81
Jolene Holthusen	Roseau High School	13
Natalie Homa	Webster Magnet School	98
Johnny Howard	Chelsea Heights Elementary School	49
Javon Jackson	Parkway Elementary School	66
Jacob Jensen	Oak Ridge Elementary School	5
Angela K. Johnson	Battle Lake High School	90
Virginia Johnson's Class	Parkway Elementary School	8
Virginia Johnson's Class	Parkway Elementary School	11
Andrew Karst	Gordon Bailey Elementary School	30
Ashley Thomas Kjos	Oak Ridge Elementary School	118
Deon Klein	Parkway Elementary School	105
Nicole Kliber	Lakeview Elementary School	138
Matt Klug	Caledonia Junior High School	31
Beth Knudsen	Heart of the Lakes Elementary School	83
Josh LaFond	Perham High School	107
Pacho Lara	Central Middle School	77
Olivia Latimer	Warba Elementary School	37
Mai Lee	Hayden Heights Elementary School	16
Peter Majerle	Central Middle School	82
Teresa March	Long Prairie High School	60
Maggie McCormack	Willmar Junior High School	80
Heidi McKay	Barnum Elementary School	119
Liam McNally	Oltman Junior High School	100
Kelly Michels	Le Sueur/Henderson Junior/Senior High School	121
Jamie Miller	Parkway Elementary School	115
Margaret Mogck's Class	North End Elementary School	106
Travis Morrison	Gordon Bailey Elementary School	57
Hnou Moua	Parkway Elementary School	109

Henry Mundstock	Pilot Knob Elementary School..................111
Bernadette Murphy	Pullman Elementary School.......................93
Betsy Murphy	Blue Earth Elementary School 108
Jon Nelson	Bemidji High School..................................32
Shannon Nibbe	Alternative Learning Center 104
Mike Olson	Highwood Hills Elementary School............48
Tyler Olson	Crestview Elementary School.....................26
Kim Oster	Aquila Primary Center.............................133
Eric Paul	Long Prairie High School 18
Lolly Pederson's Class	Parkway Elementary School 74
Terra Pehl	Mahtomedi Middle School........................78
Marie Pogotschnik	Holdingford Elementary School 34
Becky Raasch	Willmar High School 67
Ryan Rasmussen	Eisenhower Elementary School 53
Shannon Rawson	Mounds Park All Nations School..............112
Ann Reidell's Class	Parkway Elementary School 123
Jacob Richards	Wadena-Deer Creek Elementary School ..124
Kelly Ritter	Birch Grove Elementary School 17
Dustin Rosel	Southland Middle School 122
David Saniti	Edgerton Elementary School 45
Kristi Schneider	Christa McAuliffe Elementary School.......137
Anya Scholl	Worthington Area Junior High School 127
Shannon Schulte	Caledonia Elementary School..................136
Jeff Sellman	Wadena-Deer Creek Elementary School ..124
Bryan Shattuck	Chelsea Heights Elementary School..........135
Louis Smeby	Pullman Elementary School.....................134
Kira Levine Smith	Webster Magnet School 6
Songwriting Group	Wellcome Memorial Middle School 129
Tanya Starinets	Hopkins West Junior High School..............22
Tara Stuntebeck	Wadena-Deer Creek Elementary School ..124
Kyle Swanson	Oltman Junior High School......................110
Sai Thao	Parkway Elementary School 23
Heather Tichy	Wadena-Deer Creek Elementary School ..124
Devin M. Tkachuck	Mounds Park All Nations School................87
Earl Tourville	Royal Oaks Elementary School 70
Al Tripp's Class	Rush City School.......................................62
Erin Troutfetter	Gatewood Elementary School 140

Ryan Underbakke	Harriet Bishop Elementary School 27
Devon Urbanski	Madison Elementary School 41
Alex Vang	Parkway Elementary School 7
Jennifer Warren	Tanglen Elementary School 2
Becky Weets	KMS High School 75
Joel Wertheimi	Meadowbrook Elementary School 76
Anna Williams	Richfield Intermediate School 97
Beth Williams	Glen Lake Elementary School 71
Jennifer Workman	Middleton Elementary School 99
Monica Wright	North End Elementary School 47
Debbie Xiong	Parkway Elementary School 4
Mai Xiong	Parkway Elementary School 29
Jong Yang	Chelsea Heights Elementary School 10

School Index

Alice Smith Elementary School
Alternative Learning Center
Aquila Primary Center
Aquila Primary Center
Aquila Primary Center
Barnum Elementary School
Battle Lake High School
Bemidji Senior High School
Birch Grove Elementary School
Birch Grove Elementary School
Blake Middle School
Blake Middle School
Blue Earth Elementary School
Caledonia Elementary School
Caledonia Junior High School
Callaway Elementary School
Central Middle School
Central Middle School
Chelsea Heights Elementary School
Chelsea Heights Elementary School
Chelsea Heights Elementary School
Chelsea Heights Elementary School
Chelsea Heights Elementary School
Chelsea Heights Elementary School
Christa McAuliffe Elementary School
Crestview Elementary School
Edgerton Elementary School
Eisenhower Elementary School
Elk River High School
Elm Creek Elementary School
Gatewood Elementary School
GFW Middle School
Glen Lake Elementary School
Goodview Elementary School
Gordon Bailey Elementary School

Greg Hegedus 33
Shannon Nibbe 104
Timmy Babatz 40
Jessica Gruenberg 24
Kim Oster 133
Heidi McKay 119
Angela K. Johnson 90
Jon Nelson 32
Dena Gruber 94
Kelly Ritter 17
Anna Curtis 42
Aisha Ghanchi 36
Betsy Murphy 108
Shannon Schulte 136
Matt Klug 31
Lance Collman 15
Pacho Lara 77
Peter Majerle 82
Courtnie Dornfeld 3
Luther Flagstad 44
Sothara Has 92
Johnny Howard 49
Bryan Shattuck 135
Jong Yang 10
Kristi Schneider 137
Tyler Olson 26
David Saniti 45
Ryan Rasmussen 53
Jason Bistodeau 56
Sara Ennen 28
Erin Troutfetter 140
Jan Gitter 86
Beth Williams 71
Colleen Hendrick 125
Andrew Karst 30

Gordon Bailey Elementary School	Travis Morrison 57
Grand Rapids High School	Sara Allen 35
Harriet Bishop Elementary School	Ryan Underbakke............27
Hayden Heights Elementary School	Mai Lee 16
Heart of the Lakes Elementary School	Beth Knudsen 83
Hidden Oaks Middle School	Jessica DeYoung 68
Highwood Hills Elementary School	Mike Olson 48
Hillside Elementary School	Chris Collins' Class 114
Holdingford Elementary School	Marie Pogotschnik...........34
Hopkins West Junior High School	Tanya Starinets.................22
Katherine Curren Elementary School	Mary Beth D'Agosta 96
J.F. Kennedy Elementary School	Nicholas Crisp 55
Kingsland Elementary School	Kristi Hamlin 25
KMS High School	Becky Weets....................75
Lakeview Elementary School	Kelly Crandall 120
Lakeview Elementary School	Nicole Kliber 138
Le Sueur/Henderson Junior/Senior High School	Kelly Michels 121
Long Prairie High School	Teresa March...................60
Long Prairie High School	Eric Paul 18
Madison Elementary School	Devon Urbanski...............41
Mahtomedi Middle School	Terra Pehl.......................78
Meadowbrook Elementary School	Joel Wertheim 76
Middleton Elementary School	Jennifer Workman 99
Mounds Park All Nations School	Shannon Rawson...........112
Mounds Park All Nations School	Devin M. Tkachuck.........87
North End Elementary School	Monica Wright 47
North End Elementary School	Darla Heil's Class 128
North End Elementary School	Margaret Mogck's Class..106
Oak Ridge Elementary School	Jacob Jensen......................5
Oak Ridge Elementary School	Ashley Thomas Kjos.......118
Oltman Junior High School	James Adamiak.................72
Oltman Junior High School	Keith Brown....................46
Oltman Junior High School	Cory Gross....................139
Oltman Junior High School	Stephanie Hickman..........81
Oltman Junior High School	Liam McNally................100
Oltman Junior High School	Kyle Swanson 110

Parkway Elementary School	Andy Acuff 12
Parkway Elementary School	Diane Arvidson's Class 9
Parkway Elementary School	Robert Axberg's Class 101
Parkway Elementary School	Yen Dang 95
Parkway Elementary School	Landis-Arvelia Harwell 69
Parkway Elementary School	Javon Jackson 66
Parkway Elementary School	Virginia Johnson's Class 8
Parkway Elementary School	Virginia Johnson's Class.... 11
Parkway Elementary School	Deon Klein 105
Parkway Elementary School	Jamie Miller 115
Parkway Elementary School	Hnou Moua 109
Parkway Elementary School	Lolly Pederson's Class 74
Parkway Elementary School	Ann Reidell's Class 123
Parkway Elementary School	Sai Thao 23
Parkway Elementary School	Alex Vang 7
Parkway Elementary School	Debbie Xiong 4
Parkway Elementary School	Mai Xiong 29
Perham High School	Josh LaFond 107
Pilot Knob Elementary School	Henry Mundstock 111
Pine Hill Elementary School	Mike Bradley 52
Plymouth Creek Elementary School	Sarah Connelly 73
Prior Lake High School	Brian Harms 38
Pullman Elementary School	Joe Burns 43
Pullman Elementary School	Bernadette Murphy 93
Pullman Elementary School	Louis Smeby 134
Richfield Intermediate School	Anna Williams 97
Roseau High School	Jolene Holthusen 13
Royal Oaks Elementary School	Earl Tourville 70
Rush City School	Al Tripp's Class 62
St. Michael Elementary School	Amanda Grachek 50
Southland Middle School	Dustin Rosel 122
Stillwater High School	Rachel Beck 54
Stillwater Junior High School	Erica Gilberg 14
Swanville Public Schools	Nicole Borgert 84
Swanville Public Schools	Emily Gamble 131
Tanglen Elementary School	Jennifer Warren 2
Wadena-Deer Creek Elementary School	Jacob Richards 124

Wadena-Deer Creek Elementary School	Jeff Sellman......................124
Wadena-Deer Creek Elementary School	Tara Stuntebeck..............124
Wadena-Deer Creek Elementary School	Heather Tichy.................124
Warba Elementary School	Olivia Latimer...................37
Weaver Elementary School	Jesse Bewley......................59
Weaver Elementary School	Amber Goetzke 58
Webster Magnet School	Edward Burch, Jr. 132
Webster Magnet School	Natalie Homa 98
Webster Magnet School	Kira Levine Smith...............6
Wellcome Memorial Middle School	Songwriting Group 129
Willmar Junior High School	Maggie McCormack.........80
Willmar High School	Becky Raasch 67
Worthington Area Junior High School	Anya Scholl.....................127

Program Writers 1992–1993

Sigrid Bergie
John Caddy
Florence Chard Dacey
Carol Dines
Margot Fortunato Galt
Dana Jensen
Syl Jones
Gita Kar
Judith Katz
Roseann Lloyd
Charlie Maguire
Jaime Meyer
John Minczeski
Beverly Acuff Momoi
Jim Northrup, Jr.
Sheila O'Connor
Joe Paddock
Mary Rockcastle
Richard Solly
Deborah Stein
Susan Marie Swanson